I0448445

August 2013

INTELLECTUAL PROPERTY

Assessing Factors That Affect Patent Infringement Litigation Could Help Improve Patent Quality

GAO Highlights

Highlights of GAO-13-465, a report to congressional committees

INTELLECTUAL PROPERTY

Assessing Factors That Affect Patent Infringement Litigation Could Help Improve Patent Quality

Why GAO Did This Study

Legal commentators, technology companies, Congress, and others have raised questions about patent infringement lawsuits by entities that own patents but do not make products. Such entities may include universities licensing patents developed by university research, companies focused on licensing patents they developed, or companies that buy patents from others for the purposes of asserting the patents for profit.

Section 34 of AIA mandated that GAO conduct a study on the consequences of patent litigation by NPEs. This report examines (1) the volume and characteristics of recent patent litigation activity; (2) views of stakeholders knowledgeable in patent litigation on key factors that have contributed to recent patent litigation; (3) what developments in the judicial system may affect patent litigation; and (4) what actions, if any, PTO has recently taken that may affect patent litigation in the future. GAO reviewed relevant laws, analyzed patent infringement litigation data from 2000 to 2011, and interviewed officials from PTO and knowledgeable stakeholders, including representatives of companies involved in patent litigation.

What GAO Recommends

GAO recommends that PTO consider examining trends in patent infringement litigation and consider linking this information to internal patent examination data to improve patent quality and examination. PTO commented on a draft of this report and agreed with key findings and this recommendation.

View GAO-13-465. For more information, contact Frank Rusco at (202) 512-3841 or ruscof@gao.gov.

What GAO Found

From 2000 to 2010, the number of patent infringement lawsuits in the federal courts fluctuated slightly, and from 2010 to 2011, the number of such lawsuits increased by about a third. Some stakeholders GAO interviewed said that the increase in 2011 was most likely influenced by the anticipation of changes in the 2011 Leahy-Smith America Invents Act (AIA), which made several significant changes to the U.S. patent system, including limiting the number of defendants in a lawsuit, causing some plaintiffs that would have previously filed a single lawsuit with multiple defendants to break the lawsuit into multiple lawsuits. In addition, GAO's detailed analysis of a representative sample of 500 lawsuits from 2007 to 2011 shows that the number of overall defendants in patent infringement lawsuits increased by about 129 percent over this period. These data also show that companies that make products brought most of the lawsuits and that nonpracticing entities (NPE) brought about a fifth of all lawsuits. GAO's analysis of these data also found that lawsuits involving software-related patents accounted for about 89 percent of the increase in defendants over this period.

Stakeholders knowledgeable in patent litigation identified three key factors that likely contributed to many recent patent infringement lawsuits. First, several stakeholders GAO interviewed said that many such lawsuits are related to the prevalence of patents with unclear property rights; for example, several of these stakeholders noted that software-related patents often had overly broad or unclear claims or both. Second, some stakeholders said that the potential for large monetary awards from the courts, even for ideas that make only small contributions to a product, can be an incentive for patent owners to file infringement lawsuits. Third, several stakeholders said that the recognition by companies that patents are a more valuable asset than once assumed may have contributed to recent patent infringement lawsuits.

The judicial system is implementing new initiatives to improve the handling of patent cases in the federal courts, including (1) a patent pilot program, to encourage the enhancement of expertise in patent cases among district court judges, and (2) new rules in some federal court districts that are designed to reduce the time and expense of patent infringement litigation. Recent court decisions may also affect how monetary awards are calculated, among other things. Several stakeholders said that it is too early to tell what effect these initiatives will have on patent litigation.

The U.S. Patent and Trademark Office (PTO) has taken several recent actions that are likely to affect patent quality and litigation in the future, including agency initiatives and changes required by AIA. For example, in November 2011, PTO began working with the software industry to develop more uniform terminology for software-related patents. PTO officials said that they generally try to adapt to developments in patent law and industry to improve patent quality. However, the agency does not currently use information on patent litigation in initiating such actions; some PTO staff said that the types of patents involved in infringement litigation could be linked to PTO's internal data on the patent examination process, and a 2003 National Academies study showed that such analysis could be used to improve patent quality and examination by exposing patterns in the examination of patents that end up in court.

_____ United States Government Accountability Office

Contents

Abbreviations

AIA	Leahy-Smith America Invents Act
AIPLA	American Intellectual Property Law Association
AOUSC	Administrative Office of the U.S. Courts
CPC	Cooperative Patent Classification
EPO	European Patent Office
FTC	Federal Trade Commission
ITC	International Trade Commission
NPE	nonpracticing entities
PAE	patent assertion entities
PME	patent monetization entities
PTO	Patent and Trademark Office
R&D	research and development
SEC	Securities and Exchange Commission

August 22, 2013

Congressional Committees

History is filled with examples of successful inventors who did not develop products based on the technologies they patented. For example, Elias Howe patented a key component of the sewing machine—a mechanism for making a lockstitch—but it was Isaac Singer who most successfully brought these machines into the homes of thousands of Americans by obtaining crucial patents of his own and paying Howe and other inventors to license the technology described in their patents.[1] In the United States, the party that owns a patent—the patent owner—is not required to put the patent to use in order to profit from it; he can also license others to use it.[2] In some instances, patent owners may need to actively assert their patents in an adversarial context if another firm's product infringes their patents.[3] For example, Singer initially refused to obtain a license to Howe's patent, but when Howe sued Singer for infringing his patent, the two parties ultimately entered a licensing agreement.[4]

---

[1]A patent is an exclusive right granted for a fixed period of time to someone who invents or discovers (1) a new and useful process, machine, manufacture, or composition of matter or (2) any new and useful improvement of such items.

[2]In this report, when we use the term "patent owner," it includes the real party in interest when that party is not the patent owner. A real party in interest may be, among other things, an entity that has a legal right to enforce the patent, such as a parent entity or exclusive licensee.

[3]Anyone who makes, sells, offers to sell, uses, or imports the patented invention during the term of the patent without the patent owner's permission infringes the patent. Patent infringement is a strict liability offense—the alleged infringer's intent to copy or act of copying the patented invention are not relevant to the outcome of an infringement lawsuit—so an individual who independently develops an invention that falls within the scope of a patent may infringe the patent. A patent owner can grant permission to use a patented invention by licensing others to use, make, sell, or import the patented invention. Patent owners can also transfer title to their patents by assigning their patent rights to others.

[4]For more information on the dispute between Howe and Singer, see: Adam Mossof, *The Rise and Fall of the First American Patent Thicket: The Sewing Machine War of the 1850s*, 53 Ariz. L. Rev.165 (2011). See also Ryan L. Lampe & Petra Moser, *Do Patent Pools Encourage Innovation? Evidence from the 19th-Century Sewing Machine Industry*, NBER Working Paper No. 15061 (June 2009).

According to economists who have studied these issues, the U.S. patent system—authorized by the U.S. Constitution—aims to promote innovation by making it more profitable.[5] For example, a patent owner can generally exclude others from making, using, selling, or importing the patented technology for 20 years from the date on which the application for the patent was filed. By restricting competition, patents can allow their owners to earn greater profits on their patented technologies than they could earn if these technologies could be imitated freely. Due to the exclusive rights provided by patents, patents can help their owners recoup the costs of the research and development (R&D) of new technologies. On the other hand, any limiting effects on competition caused by the exclusive nature of patents may result in higher prices for products having patented technologies. The patent system, therefore, gives rise to complex trade-offs involving innovation and competition. These trade-offs can be affected by decisions made by the United States Patent and Trademark Office (PTO), which issues patents; the federal courts, which decide patent infringement lawsuits; and the International Trade Commission (ITC), which can order imports that infringe U.S. patents to be excluded from entering the country.

In addition to individual inventors who may choose not to develop products based on their patents, there are other types of "nonpracticing" patent owners, or nonpracticing entities (NPE). For example, some universities are NPEs, as they develop technologies in campus laboratories, and rather than producing and selling products that incorporate these technologies, they license their patents on these technologies to companies who use them in their products. In addition, some private firms are NPEs as they specialize in R&D, and rather than selling products, they license the patents for those products to fund further research. Some NPEs simply buy patents from others for the purpose of asserting them for profit; these NPEs are known as patent monetization entities (PME).[6] Other PMEs include companies that produced products at one time and still own patents on the technologies

---

[5]The Constitution grants to Congress the power "[t]o promote the Progress of Science and useful Arts, by securing for limited Times to Authors and Inventors the exclusive Right to their respective Writings and Discoveries." U.S. Const., art. I, § 8, cl. 8.

[6]The Federal Trade Commission uses the related term "patent assertion entities" to focus on entities whose business model solely focuses on asserting typically purchased patents. As such, the PME term also encompasses entities that might use third-party NPEs to assert patents for them.

for those products. Experts agree that NPEs have a variety of business models, which makes it difficult to fit them neatly into any one of these categories. For example, even companies that produce products related to their patents—known as practicing patent owners, or operating companies—sometimes assert patents that they own but that are not related to the products they produce, which further complicates defining an NPE.

Some legal commentators, technology companies, the Federal Trade Commission (FTC),[7] and Congress, among others, have raised concerns that patent infringement litigation by NPEs is increasing and that this litigation, in some cases, has imposed high costs on firms that are actually developing and manufacturing products, especially in the software and technology sectors. Among the concerns of some technology companies and legal commentators is that because NPEs generally face lower litigation costs than those they are accusing of infringement, NPEs are likely to use the threat of imposing these costs as leverage in seeking infringement compensation.[8] These technology companies and legal commentators also have noted that NPEs often claim that their patent covers an entire technology when in fact it may cover just a small improvement in an existing technology, and that it can be difficult for judges and juries to determine the patent's scope when complex technologies are involved.

The Leahy-Smith America Invents Act (AIA), signed into law September 16, 2011, made several significant changes to the U.S. patent system. Section 34 of the AIA[9] mandates that GAO conduct a study on the

---

[7]FTC's mission includes prevention of and enforcement against anticompetitive, unfair, or deceptive business practices including, potentially, patent assertion activities.

[8]This is not unique to patent infringement litigation. As discussed later in the report, in civil lawsuits, the parties must exchange certain information relevant to the litigation, a process known as discovery. Discovery costs in complex litigation, including patent infringement litigation, can run into the millions of dollars. Because NPEs do not make products, they generally have less information to disclose and thus have lower discovery costs. They also cannot be countersued for patent infringement. This asymmetry in litigation costs (which exists in other types of complex litigation) can give NPEs leverage in seeking financial compensation from operating companies.

[9]Pub. L. No.112-29 § 34 (2011).

consequences of patent litigation by NPEs.[10] Our objectives in conducting this study were to determine: (1) what is known about the volume and characteristics of recent patent litigation activity; (2) the views of stakeholders knowledgeable in patent litigation on what is known about the key factors that have contributed to recent patent litigation; (3) what developments in the judicial system may affect patent litigation; and (4) what actions, if any, has PTO recently taken that may affect patent litigation in the future.

To address all four objectives, we reviewed relevant laws, including the AIA, and interviewed officials from PTO, FTC, ITC, and 44 stakeholders knowledgeable about patent litigation. These included representatives from companies and industry groups that were recently sued for patent infringement, PMEs, judges, various legal commentators (including law professors and patent litigators representing operating companies and PMEs), economists, representatives from research universities that license patents, patent brokers who help others buy and sell patents, venture capitalists, and individual inventors.[11] To describe what is known about the volume and characteristics of recent patent litigation activity for 2007 to 2011, we analyzed patent infringement litigation data from Lex Machina, a firm that collects and analyzes data on patent litigation. Lex Machina provided data for all patent infringement lawsuits filed in federal district court from 2000 to 2011. From these data, Lex Machina selected a random, generalizable sample of 500 lawsuits (100 per year from 2007 to 2011), which allows us to estimate percentages with a margin of error of

---

[10]As noted in a September 7, 2011, letter from the Comptroller General to the chairs and ranking members of the congressional committees with jurisdiction over patents, the bill being considered at that time would have required a GAO study involving several questions for which reliable data were not available or could not be obtained. The bill was enacted without change, but the Chair of the Senate Judiciary Committee, responding to these concerns, stated that GAO should note data and methodology limitations in its report prepared in response to the mandate. 157 CONG. REC. S 5402, S5441 (daily ed. Sept. 8, 2011) (statement of Sen. Leahy). Consequently, we developed report objectives consistent with these limitations, and we have noted specific data limitations in appendix I and throughout this report, as appropriate.

[11]We identified some of these stakeholders from patent infringement litigation data from 2000 through 2011 that we reviewed. Representatives of companies and PMEs we talked with had regularly been sued or had regularly sued others over the past decade. Other stakeholders we identified through our review of academic literature on patent litigation and the patent system and were knowledgeable in the issues we were asked to study. Because stakeholders varied in their expertise with various topics, not every stakeholder provided an opinion on every topic.

no more than plus or minus 5 percentage points over all these years and no more than plus or minus 10 percentage points for any particular year.[12] Lex Machina used a variety of characteristics from court records, U.S. Securities and Exchange Commission (SEC) filings, and corporate websites to categorize litigants, including as an operating company or likely operating company, PME or likely PME, university, or an individual or trust.[13] A limitation of this categorization is that litigants were not contacted to verify their identity, so there is some uncertainty about the accuracy of the category in which Lex Machina placed them. We also obtained patent infringement data from RPX, another firm that collects data on patent infringement lawsuits, in an effort to verify Lex Machina's litigant categorizations.[14] Also to describe what is known about the volume and characteristics of recent patent litigation activity, we reported data collected by the American Intellectual Property Law Association

---

[12]This sample allowed us to draw conclusions about the broader population of patent infringement lawsuits for each of these years and is therefore generalizable to all patent infringement lawsuits filed in federal district court from 2007 to 2011. However, as noted, estimates from the Lex Machina sample are subject to a 5 percent margin of error. This means that an estimate of 50 percent, for example, based on all years of data, would have a 95 percent confidence interval of between 45 percent and 55 percent. The margin of error is 10 percent when looking at individual years, which means that an estimate of 50 percent, for example, looking at an individual year, would have a 95 percent confidence interval of between 40 percent and 60 percent. Because Lex Machina followed a probability procedure based on random selections, the sample is only one of a large number of samples that might have been drawn. Since each sample could have provided different estimates, we express our confidence in the precision of our particular sample's results as a 95 percent confidence interval. This is the interval that would contain the actual population value for 95 percent of the samples that could have been drawn. Unless otherwise noted, the margin of error associated with the confidence intervals of our survey estimates is no more than plus or minus 10 percentage points at the 95 percent level of confidence.

[13]Definitions of these categories are discussed below and detailed in appendix I. We found that it was difficult to reliably identify the type of NPEs through analysis of data from court records because, among other things, firms do not identify themselves as such in these records. Lex Machina did not include patent owners that primarily seek to develop and transfer technology, such as universities and research firms, as PMEs. See appendix I for more detail on Lex Machina's categorizations and our review of them.

[14]RPX also purchases patents itself, to prevent them from being asserted against its members. RPX provided us with summary data on the number of patent infringement lawsuits filed in federal district court since January 2005. RPX's data identified NPEs and other types of plaintiffs in these lawsuits by using a variety of factors, such as whether there was evidence that an entity sells or develops products. RPX representatives said that they used professional judgment to some extent in making these determinations. We were not able to fully assess the reliability of the judgments RPX used in making these classifications.

(AIPLA) on the costs of patent litigation.[15] We also reviewed academic literature on patent litigation and the patent system in general and assessed the methodology of the studies we reported on for soundness. To assess the reliability of data from Lex Machina, we met with Lex Machina staff, examined documentation, and tested and reviewed the data provided for completeness and accuracy. To assess the reliability of data from PTO, AIPLA, and RPX, we conducted interviews and reviewed relevant methodology documentation. We found these data to be sufficiently reliable for purposes of this report.

In addition to the steps we took to address all four objectives, in order to describe views of stakeholders on what is known about the key factors that contribute to recent patent litigation trends, we reviewed academic literature on the patent and judicial systems and the benefits and costs of patent assertion, including economic and legal studies. To describe developments in the judicial system that may affect patent litigation, we interviewed officials and judges from the U.S. District Courts for the District of Delaware and for the Eastern District of Texas. We selected these district courts because they had high levels of patent infringement lawsuits according to Lex Machina data. We also interviewed judges with the U.S. Court of Appeals for the Federal Circuit (Federal Circuit) in Washington, D.C., which hears appeals of patent cases decided in federal district courts, as well as officials from the Administrative Office of the U.S. Courts (AOUSC) and the Federal Judicial Center—organizations that provide broad administrative, legal, and technological services and support to the judicial branch. We also reviewed documents and data from the courts, as well as economic and legal studies. To describe what actions, if any, PTO has recently taken that may affect patent litigation in the future, we conducted interviews with officials from PTO and reviewed documents and data from the agency, as well as economic and legal studies. Appendix I provides more details on our scope and methodology.

We conducted this performance audit from November 2011 to August 2013 in accordance with generally accepted government auditing standards. Those standards require that we plan and perform the audit to

[15]AIPLA is a national, voluntary bar association constituted primarily of patent lawyers in private and corporate practice, in government service, and in the academic community. See AIPLA, *Report of the Economic Survey 2011* (Arlington, Va.: July 2011). AIPLA surveyed its members during 2011 and asked them to estimate legal costs for typical patent infringement cases. AIPLA's findings are based on an 18 percent response rate.

obtain sufficient, appropriate evidence to provide a reasonable basis for our findings and conclusions based on our audit objectives. We believe that the evidence obtained provides a reasonable basis for our findings and conclusions based on our audit objectives.

Background

When PTO receives a patent application, it assigns it to a team of patent examiners with relevant technology expertise. PTO does not begin examining patent applications upon receiving them and PTO's data shows that, as of June 2013, the average time between filing and an examiner's initial decision on the application was about 18 months.[16] On average, it takes 30 months for PTO to issue a patent once an application is submitted.

The focus of patent examination is determining whether the patent application satisfies the statutory requirements for a patent, including: (1) novelty, (2) nonobviousness, (3) utility, and (4) patentable subject matter.[17] Generally, other patents, publications, and publicly disclosed but unpatented inventions that pre-date the patent application's filing date are known as prior art. During patent examination, the examiner, among other things, compares an application's claims to the prior art to determine whether the claimed invention is novel and nonobvious.[18] The examiner then decides to reject or grant the claims in the application and deny the application or grant a patent.

U.S. patents include the specification and the claims:

[16]PTO's data show that the current inventory of new applications that have not yet received an initial decision was around 600,000 applications. PTO refers to these initial decisions as a "first action on the merits."

[17]To be patentable subject matter, the invention must be a (1) process; (2) machine; (3) manufacture; (4) composition of matter; or (5) improvement of a process, machine, manufacture, or composition of matter. To be nonobvious, the claimed invention's improvements to the prior art must be more than the predictable use of prior art elements according to their established functions. Specifically, at the time of the invention, the differences between the scope and content of claimed invention and the prior art cannot render the claimed invention as a whole obvious to a person having ordinary skill in the art.

[18]During the patent examination, the applicant and the examiner communicate about the application, including aspects that might be deficient. For example, the examiner may inform the applicant that one of the claims is not novel because of prior art, and the applicant might revise the claim to distinguish it from the prior art the examiner found.

GAO-13-465 Patent Litigation

- The specification is a written description of the invention that, among other things, sufficiently discloses the invention and the manner and process of making and using it. The specification must be written in full, clear, concise, and exact terms so as to enable any person skilled in the art to make and use the invention. As an example, an excerpt from the specification for a cardboard coffee cup and insulator invention describes "corrugated containers and container holders which can be made from existing cellulosic materials, such as paper."
- The claims define the scope of the invention for which protection is granted and must be definite. There are often a dozen or more claims per patent, and they can often be difficult for a layperson to understand, according to legal commentators. For example, one claim for the cardboard coffee cup insulator begins by referring to "a recyclable, insulating beverage container holder, comprising a corrugated tubular member comprising cellulosic material and at least a first opening therein for receiving and retaining a beverage container." A patent's claims can be written broadly or be more narrowly defined, according to legal commentators, and applicants can change the wording of claims—which can affect their scope—during examination based on examiner feedback. Patents are a property right and—like land—their claims define their boundaries. When a property right is not clearly defined, it can lead to boundary disputes, although to some extent uncertainty is inherent. Consequently, legal commentators define high-quality patents as those whose claims clearly define and provide clear notice of their boundaries.

Once issued by PTO, a patent is presumed to be valid. However, the patentability of its claims can be challenged in administrative proceedings before PTO or its Patent Trial and Appeal Board and its validity can be challenged in federal court. For example, the AIA established three new administrative proceedings for entities to challenge the patentability of a patent's claims:

- Inter partes review.[19] This proceeding allows anyone who is not the patent owner to request review of an issued patent by presenting prior art to PTO—either patents or other publications—to challenge the claimed invention's patentability as obvious or not novel. This review proceeding became available on September 16, 2012, 1 year after the enactment of the AIA, but entities cannot request this review until the

---

[19]Inter partes is Latin for "between the parties."

later of (1) 9 months after a patent is granted or (2) completion of post-grant review, if such a proceeding is held.

- Post-grant review. This proceeding allows anyone who is not the patent owner to request a review of an issued patent that challenges at least one of the claims' patentability in more circumstances than inter partes review—such as the invention not being useful—and not solely based on prior art. This proceeding is available for patents issued from patent applications with a filing date of March 16, 2013, or later and requests must be filed within 9 months of the patent's issuance.
- Transitional program for covered business method patents. [20] This proceeding allows anyone who is sued or charged with infringing a covered business method patent to request a review of the patent to challenge a claim's patentability in generally the same circumstances as post-grant review. This review proceeding became available on September 16, 2012, and requests must be filed within 9 months of the patent's issuance.

In addition, a patent's validity can be challenged in the 94 federal district courts throughout the country by, for example, presenting additional prior art that PTO may have been unaware of when it granted the patent. Challenges to a patent's validity are often brought by an accused infringer who has been sued for infringing the patent.[21] Patent owners can bring infringement lawsuits against anyone who uses, makes, sells, offers to sell, or imports the patented invention without authorization because a patent is a right to exclude others from practicing the invention. Exactly what a patent covers and whether another product infringes the patent's claims are rarely easy questions to resolve in litigation, according to legal commentators. As noted, appeals of district court decisions in infringement cases are heard in the U.S. Court of Appeals for the Federal Circuit in Washington D.C.

---

[20] A covered business method patent is a patent that claims a method or corresponding apparatus for performing data processing or other operations used in the practice, administration, or management of a financial product or service but does not include patents for technological inventions. This transitional program is subject to a sunset provision that will repeal the program on September 16, 2020.

[21] In patent infringement lawsuits, the accused infringer often challenges the patent's validity as an "affirmative defense," meaning that even if the infringement allegations are true, the would-be infringer is not liable because the patent is invalid. A party accused of infringement can also file a lawsuit to obtain a court decision on whether they are infringing or whether the patent is valid, which is known as a declaratory judgment action.

If a patent infringement lawsuit is not dismissed in the initial stages, it proceeds to discovery (a process that exists in all federal civil litigation) and claim construction. Discovery requires the accused infringer to produce documents or other information that shows, among other things, how the allegedly infringing product is made and operates to help the patent owner establish infringement. Similarly, the patent owner must produce documents or other information that the accused infringer can use to challenge the patent's validity, among other things. However, parties that do not offer products or services using the patents at issue often have far fewer documents to disclose—because they do not have any documents related to their products or services—than patent owners or accused infringers who do offer products or services.[22]

With this information the patent owner specifies which patent claims allegedly are infringed and the alleged infringer responds by explaining why the allegedly infringing product is not covered by the patent's claims. This identifies the patent claims the court needs to interpret. Known as claim construction, this is a fundamental issue in patent cases, and each party tries to persuade the court to interpret the patent claims in its favor. The court has broad discretion in how it goes about this process, which can involve a hearing with testimony from witnesses, according to legal commentators.[23] In addition, if the patent's validity is being challenged, the alleged infringer specifies why the patent allegedly is not valid, including any prior art.

Once the judge interprets the claims, the claims are then applied to the allegedly infringing product, to determine infringement, and to the prior art, to determine the patent's validity if it is challenged. If the patent is found to be both valid and infringed, the court can award the patent owner monetary damages, issue an injunction to prohibit further infringement, or both. The court is required to award damages adequate to compensate

---

[22] As noted, asymmetrical discovery demands, burdens, and costs are not unique to NPE patent infringement litigation. For example, parties in class actions and antitrust litigation typically face the same asymmetry. *See, e.g.,Thorogood v. Sears, Roebuck & Co.,* 624 F.3d 842, 849-50 (7th Cir. 2010) (class action discovery); *Bell Atlantic Corp. v. Twombly,* 550 U.S. 544, 558-559 (2007) (antitrust discovery).

[23]This hearing is often referred to as a *Markman* hearing after the Supreme Court's decision in *Markman v. Westview Instruments, Inc.,* 517 U.S. 370 (1996).

for the infringement that are at least what a reasonable royalty would be for the use made of the invention by the infringer.[24]

In addition to being enforced in the federal courts, patents can also be enforced at ITC, which handles investigations into allegations of certain unfair practices in import trade. Specifically, certain patent owners can file a complaint with ITC if imported goods infringe their patent or are made by a process covered by the patent's claims.[25] If ITC determines after an investigation that an imported good infringes a patent, the agency can issue an exclusion order barring the products at issue from entry into the United States, which the President can disapprove for policy reasons. ITC decisions can be appealed to the U.S. Court of Appeals for the Federal Circuit. Legal commentators have reported that a 2006 Supreme Court decision led to increased complaints alleging imported goods infringed U.S. patents being filed with ITC, and recent ITC data show that the number of investigations instituted by ITC increased from 32 in 2006 to 37 in 2012.[26]

According to PTO data, applications for all types of patents have increased in recent years, and patents granted for software-related technologies have seen dramatic increases over the past 2 decades (see

---

[24]The judge has the authority to increase damages up to three times the amount initially awarded, called treble damages, for cases of willful infringement. In "exceptional cases" the court is authorized to award the prevailing party reasonable attorney fees.

[25]In order for ITC to have jurisdiction to hear the complaint, there must be an industry in the United States in existence or in the process of being established that relates to the articles protected by the patent concerned. An industry in the United States is considered to exist if there is in the country, with respect to the articles protected by the patent: (1) a significant investment in plant and equipment; (2) significant employment of labor or capital; or (3) substantial investment in its exploitation, including engineering, research and development, or licensing. This is known as the domestic industry requirement.

[26]Prior to this 2006 Supreme Court case, the Federal Circuit's general rule was for district court judges to issue injunctions in patent cases once validity and infringement had been determined except in unusual cases under exceptional circumstances and in rare instances to protect public interest. In the 2006 eBay decision, the Supreme Court ruled that district courts should not assume an injunction was automatically needed in patent infringement cases and instead should use the same test used in other cases to determine whether to award the plaintiff an injunction. *eBay, Inc. v. MercExchange, L.L.C.*, 547 U.S. 388 (2006). According to several legal commentators we spoke with, this decision has generally made it more difficult for NPEs to obtain injunctions in the courts and has led them to pursue exclusion orders at ITC—although there may have been other reasons for the increase in filings, including the relative speed of proceedings at ITC.

fig. 1).[27] Software-related patents occur in a variety of technologies containing at least some element of software, and cover things like sending messages or conducting business over the Internet (e.g. e-commerce). Patents related to software can, but do not generally, detail computer software programming code in the specification, but often provide a more general description of the invention, which can be programmed in a variety of ways.

Figure 1: Number of Software-Related Patents Granted per Year by PTO, 1991 to 2011

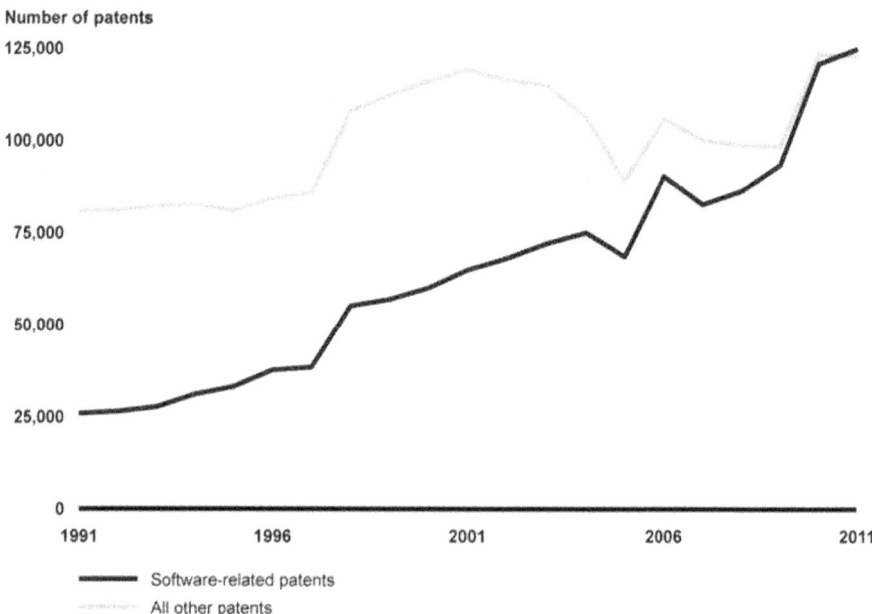

Source: GAO analysis of United States Patent and Trademark Office data

Note: Software-related patents include a number of patent classes that are most likely to include patents with software-related claims, and this includes business method patents.

According to legal commentators, the number of software-related patents grew as computers were integrated into a greater expanse of everyday

---

[27]Although PTO does not have a specific "software-related" patent class, we combined a number of entire patent classes that PTO economists have said are most likely to include patents with software-related claims, and this includes business method patents. For the list of these classes, see S. Graham, , and S. Vishnubhakat, *Of Smart Phone Wars and Software Patents,* Journal of Economic Perspectives, v. 27 no.1 (2013), pp. 67-86.

products. By 2011 patents related to software made up more than half of all issued patents. Software was not always patentable, and Supreme Court decisions in the 1970s found mathematical formulas used by computers were not patentable subject matter.[28] However, a 1981 Supreme Court decision overturned PTO's denial of a patent application for a mathematical formula and a programmed digital computer because, as a process, it was patentable subject matter.[29] Subsequently, in 1998, the Federal Circuit ruled that a mathematical formula in the form of a computer program is patentable if it is applied in a useful way.[30] According to PTO officials, the agency interpreted these cases as limiting their ability to reject patent applications for computer processes. Legal commentators also said that after these decisions, particularly the 1998 Federal Circuit decision, software-related patenting grew as many technology companies made the conscious effort to generate more patents for offensive or defensive purposes—that is, to use them to sue or countersue competitors in infringement lawsuits, rather than use them to recoup R&D costs. As recently as 2010, the Supreme Court has noted that the patent statute acknowledges that business methods are patentable subject matter.[31]

---

[28]*Gottschalk v. Benson*, 409 U.S. 63 (1972) (finding a mathematical formula that had no substantial practical application except in connection with a digital computer was not patentable because it is like a law of nature, which cannot be the subject of a patent); *Parker v. Flook*, 437 U.S. 584 (1978) (finding a method for updating alarm limits through computerized calculations was not patentable because the alarm limit is a number and the patent application was for a formula to compute it).

[29]*Diamond v. Diehr*, 450 U.S. 175 (1981) (finding a patent claim containing a mathematical formula that implements or applies that formula in a structure or process, which, when considered as a whole, is performing a function which the patent laws were designed to protect, to be patentable).

[30]*State Street Bank & Trust Co. v. Signature Financial Group, Inc.*, 149 F.3d 1368 (Fed. Cir. 1998).

[31]*Bilski v. Kappos*, __ U.S. __, 130 S. Ct. 3218 (2010).

Number of Patent Infringement Lawsuits Increased Significantly in 2011 and the Number of Defendants Increased between 2007 and 2011

From 2000 to 2010, the number of patent infringement lawsuits fluctuated slightly, and from 2010 to 2011, the number increased about 31 percent. Our more detailed analysis of a generalizable sample of 500 lawsuits estimates that the overall number of defendants in these cases increased from 2007 to 2011 by about 129 percent over the 5-year period. This analysis also shows that operating companies brought most of these lawsuits and that lawsuits involving software-related patents accounted for about 89 percent of the increase in defendants during this period. Some stakeholders we interviewed said that they experienced a substantial amount of patent assertion without firms ever filing lawsuits against them.

Number of Patent Infringement Lawsuits Fluctuated Slightly before Increasing in 2011, but Number of Defendants Increased from 2007 to 2011

From 2000 to 2011, about 29,000 patent infringement lawsuits were filed in U.S. district courts. The number of these lawsuits fluctuated slightly until 2011, when there was a 31 percent increase (see fig. 2).

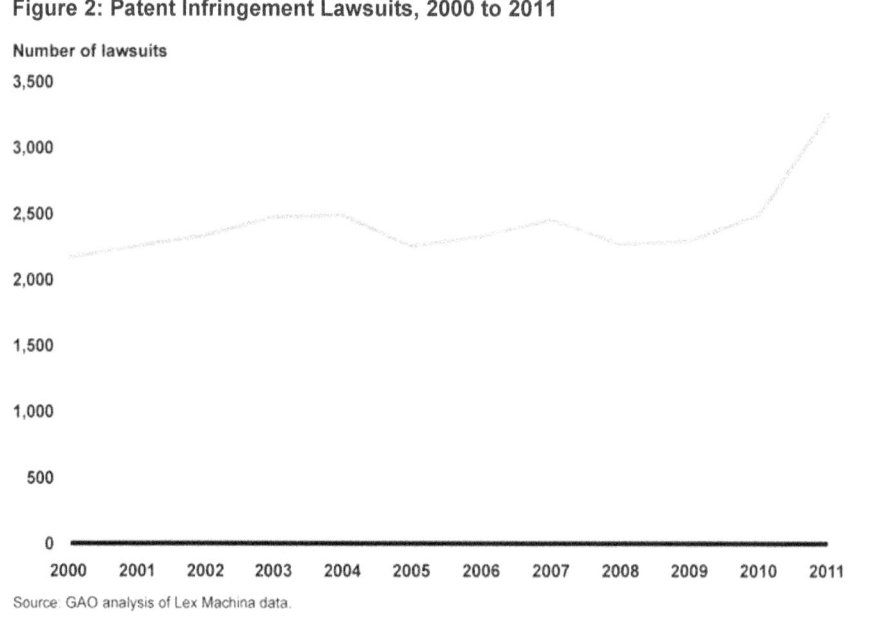

Figure 2: Patent Infringement Lawsuits, 2000 to 2011

Source: GAO analysis of Lex Machina data.

Specifically, about 900 more lawsuits were filed in 2011 than the average number of lawsuits filed in each of the previous years. Some stakeholders we interviewed generally attributed the increase in 2011 to patent owners' anticipation of the passage of AIA, which restricts the number of accused infringers who can be joined in a single lawsuit.[32] Prior to the enactment of AIA, plaintiffs could sue numerous defendants in a single lawsuit. AIA restricts this practice by prohibiting joining unrelated defendants into a single lawsuit based solely on allegations that they have infringed the same patent. According to the legislative history of AIA, this provision was designed to address problems created by plaintiffs joining defendants, sometimes numbering in the dozens.[33] As a result, some stakeholders we interviewed generally agreed that the increase in 2011 was due to the fact that plaintiffs had to file more lawsuits at the end of 2011 after AIA's enactment in order to sue the same number of defendants or anticipated this change and rushed to file lawsuits against multiple defendants before it was enacted. In addition, our analysis of a generalizable sample of data from 2007 through 2011 estimates that the number of overall defendants in patent infringement suits increased by about 129 percent over the 5-year period (see fig. 3).

---

[32]Pub. L. No. 112-29, § 19(d)(1) (2011). Specifically, accused infringers may be joined, or have their actions consolidated for trial, only if (1) questions of fact common to all will arise in the action; and (2) any right to relief is asserted against the parties jointly and severally or with respect to or arising out of the same transaction, occurrence, or series of transactions or occurrences relating to the same accused product or process. AIA Section 19(d)(1), however, allows an accused infringer to waive these restrictions.

[33]H. Rep. No. 112-98, at 54 (2011).

GAO-13-465 Patent Litigation

Figure 3: Estimated Number of Defendants in Patent Infringement Lawsuits, 2007 to 2011

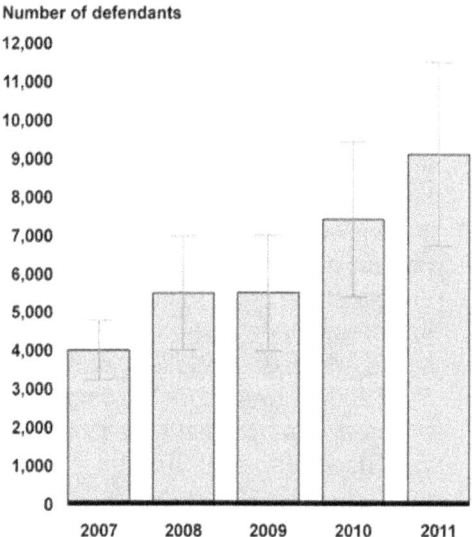

Source: GAO analysis of Lex Machina data

Note: Defendant estimates are representative of all patent infringement lawsuits and error bars display 95 percent confidence intervals.

Representatives of several operating companies that we interviewed said they are being sued more often since the mid-2000s. For example, one former official at a large technology company told us that, in 2002, the company was a defendant in five patent infringement lawsuits, but in 2011, it was a defendant in more than 50. However, a few legal commentators we interviewed said that such increases are common during periods of rapid technological change—new industries lead to more patents and the number of patent infringement lawsuits also increases because there are more patents to be enforced. Similarly, one researcher working on these issues told us that, historically, major technological developments—such as the development of automobiles, airplanes, and radio—have also led to temporary, dramatic increases in patent infringement lawsuits.

Characteristics of Plaintiffs in Recent Patent Litigation

Operating companies brought most of the patent infringement lawsuits from 2007 to 2011. According to our analysis of data for this period, operating companies and related entities brought an estimated 68 percent of all lawsuits.[34] PMEs and likely PMEs brought 19 percent of the lawsuits.[35] PMEs and likely PMEs brought 17 percent of all lawsuits in 2007 and 24 percent in 2011, although this increase was not statistically significant. In contrast, operating companies and related entities filed 76 percent of the lawsuits in 2007 and 59 percent in 2011, a statistically significant decrease.[36] Individual inventors brought about 8 percent of the lawsuits, and research firms and universities brought less than 3 percent over the 5 year span. In about 3 percent of the lawsuits there was insufficient evidence to determine the type of plaintiff (see fig. 4).

---

[34]The evidence that Lex Machina used to classify an entity as an operating company and that we then used to review Lex Machina's classifications is described in appendix I. Related entities included subsidiaries of operating companies—see appendix I for more information. We did not verify whether the companies practiced the patents at issue in the lawsuit.

[35] The evidence that Lex Machina used to classify an entity as a PME or likely PME and that we then used to review Lex Machina's classifications is described in appendix I. Another paper using data from Lex Machina presented different proportions of patent monetizing plaintiffs, and these differences may be due to differences in methodology. For example, this study included other plaintiff groups as patent monetizers, including individuals and trusts. See Robin Feldman, Tom Ewing, and Sara Jeruss, *The AIA 500 Expanded: The Effects of Patent Monetization Entities*, UCLA Journal of Law & Technology (forthcoming).

[36]Our analysis of litigation data from RPX showed similar results. Specifically, RPX's classification of all infringement suits from 2007 to 2011 shows that operating companies brought 69 percent of lawsuits, and firms that RPX classified as patent assertion entities (PAE) brought 25 percent. RPX's PAE category excluded universities and individual inventors acting as NPEs, making it similar to Lex Machina's PME category. Individual inventors brought about 6 percent of the lawsuits, and universities brought less than 1 percent. Operating companies litigating patents that do not relate to the technology of their primary business sector—classified as noncompeting entities by RPX—brought less than 1 percent of all lawsuits. Additionally, lawsuits filed by PAEs increased by about a third from 2007 to 2010 and, in 2011, doubled over the previous year, and lawsuits brought by operating companies decreased by about 6 percent from 2007 to 2010 and, in 2011, increased by about 3 percent over the previous year.

Figure 4: Estimated Patent Infringement Lawsuits by Type of Plaintiff, 2007 to 2011

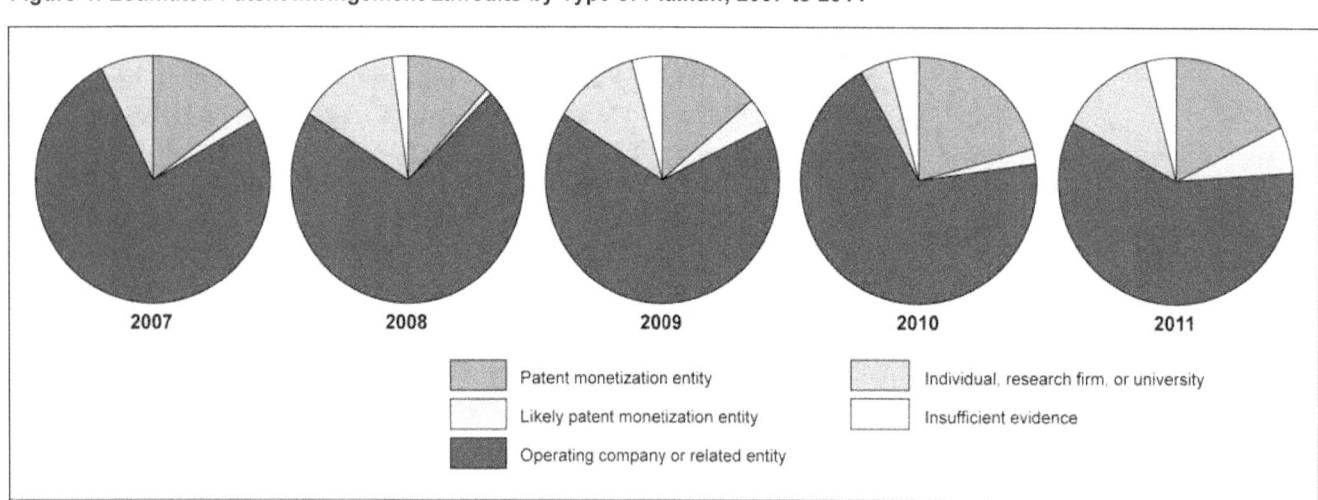

2007   2008   2009   2010   2011

- Patent monetization entity
- Likely patent monetization entity
- Operating company or related entity
- Individual, research firm, or university
- Insufficient evidence

Source: GAO analysis of Lex Machina data.

Note: Lawsuit estimates are subject to a margin of error of up to plus or minus 10 percentage points.

Our analysis of the data from 2007 through 2011 shows that PMEs tended to sue more defendants per suit than operating companies. For this period, there were about 1.9 defendants on average for suits filed by operating companies, and about 4.1 defendants on average for suits filed by PMEs. In addition, a disproportionate share of PMEs sued a relatively large number of defendants. For example, about 12 percent of PMEs sued 10 defendants or more in a single lawsuit, compared to about 3 percent of operating companies, a statistically significant difference. Thus, even with bringing about a fifth of all patent infringement lawsuits from 2007 to 2011, PMEs sued close to one-third of the overall defendants, accounting for about half of the overall increase in defendants. Additionally, the estimated total number of defendants sued by PMEs more than tripled from 834 in 2007 to 3,401 in 2011, while the increase in the total number of defendants sued by operating companies was not statistically significant.[37]

To further explore the characteristics of PMEs and other NPEs, we interviewed stakeholders knowledgeable about patent infringement lawsuits. According to some stakeholders we interviewed, NPEs have many different characteristics and there are a spectrum of NPE business models and behaviors, including operating companies that partner with NPEs to file infringement suits.[38] These different types of NPEs include the following:

- PMEs and likely PMEs. PMEs we spoke with did not develop technology or sell products but, instead, derived most of their revenue from asserting patents against operating companies. Some of these PMEs told us that they acquired patents from a variety of sellers, such as universities, individual inventors, failed companies, or operating companies. A few of these PMEs told us they were able to get patents on their own even with minimal R&D investments, especially for software-related processes. Some PMEs we spoke with said that they formerly produced patented products and now simply assert those patents, and others said that they sued on behalf of individual inventors who did not have the resources to enforce patents on their own.
- Entities Related to Operating Companies. Our analysis of patent infringement lawsuit data shows that some entities were subsidiaries of or had other corporate relationships with operating companies, although they did not produce products themselves. In addition, some stakeholders we interviewed said that operating companies sometimes partner with PMEs to monetize patents. In some cases, these partnerships may allow an operating company to sue its competitors with less risk of countersuits. A few operating companies we spoke with acknowledged that they are aware of such partnerships, although none said they engaged in this practice. The two patent brokers we interviewed told us that they have structured

---

[37]Our analysis of RPX data showed similar results. Specifically, RPX's data show that from 2007 to 2011 operating companies sued about 51 percent of all defendants and that firms RPX classified as PAEs sued about 42 percent of all defendants. Additionally, defendants sued by these firms almost tripled, while defendants sued by operating companies decreased by about 20 percent. RPX identified more than 200 NPEs that sued more than 20 defendants since 2005, suing 12 defendants per suit on average.

[38]Often both the NPE and operating company appear as plaintiffs in the same suit.

agreements where they transfer patents from an operating company to a PME, and one legal commentator who also structured such deals told us that operating companies often retain an interest in the gains from any lawsuits the PME files. This commentator also said that there are many PME lawsuits in which the identity of interested operating companies is intentionally hidden; our review of court records indicates that corporate relationships may not be easily deciphered. In some cases, business relationships were easily identifiable from court records and in other cases the links were more difficult to identify. [39] Further, some operating companies, like PMEs, also assert patents not related to products they produce, according to some stakeholders.[40]

- Research firms. Representatives from a few of the companies we interviewed said that they invested heavily in R&D and made efforts to share their technology with other companies and to help them develop new products. Specifically, these representatives told us that their companies did not focus on producing products but, rather, mainly developed new technologies and then licensed them to operating companies to pay for continued R&D.[41] These representatives also said that they provided technical support to the firms they license patents to helping them to make the best use of their patented technologies, which distinguishes them from PMEs.

- Universities. Many universities license their patented technologies to companies who use them in their products, according to a representative from each of two large research universities we spoke with, although they said that the licensing revenue is generally small in relation to other sources of university revenue. They also noted that licensing at many universities is mostly driven by life sciences research and that, sometimes before research begins, universities develop partnerships with private sector firms, such as

---

[39]For example, some operating companies owned patent monetization subsidiaries that shared their name, and others were linked to outside monetization entities with different names.

[40]RPX collects data on these types of lawsuits and, according to RPX's data, these lawsuits accounted for less than 1 percent of lawsuits in RPX's database from 2007 to 2011.

[41]These research firms told us that they file patent infringement lawsuits if their patented technologies are used without or in violation of licensing agreements. Economic literature suggests that this division of labor is valuable because companies that specialize in R&D can often innovate more nimbly and create new, innovative technologies that other companies can then incorporate into products they manufacture.

pharmaceutical companies, who have the first right to bring patented ideas into the marketplace.

Types of Patents Involved in Recent Patent Infringement Litigation

Our analysis of patent infringement lawsuit data from 2007 to 2011 shows that on average about 46 percent of the lawsuits involved software-related patents. Between 2007 to 2011, 64 percent of defendants were sued over software-related patents, and these patents were at issue in the lawsuits that accounted for about 89 percent of the increase in defendants over this period (see fig. 5). About 49 percent of the patents in our sample were asserted within 5 years of being granted, and there was no statistically significant difference between software-related patents and other patents in this regard.

Figure 5: Estimated Number of Patent Infringement Lawsuits and Defendants Associated with Software-Related Patents, 2007 to 2011

Estimated number of lawsuits

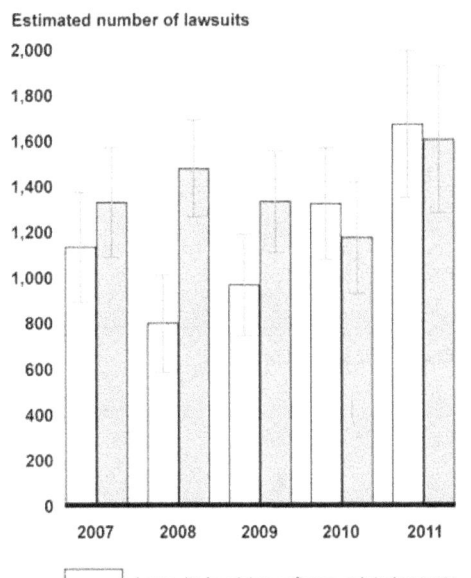

Estimated number of defendants

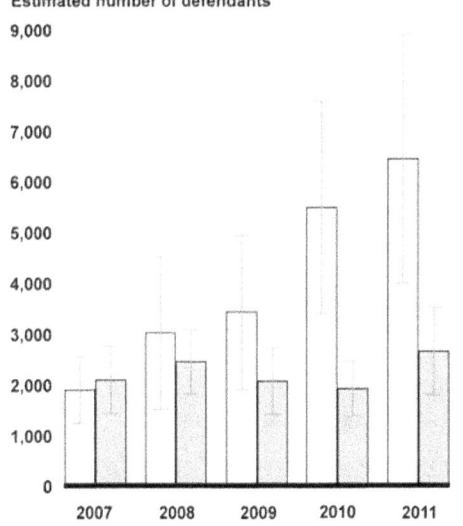

☐ Lawsuits involving software-related patents

▨ Lawsuits that do not involve software-related patents

Source: GAO analysis of Lex Machina data.

Notes: Lawsuit and defendant estimates are representative of all patent infringement lawsuits and error bars display 95 percent confidence intervals. Software-related patents include a number of patent classes that are most likely to include patents with software-related claims, and this includes business method patents.

Our analysis of patent infringement lawsuit data from 2007 to 2011 shows that operating companies and PMEs both asserted software-related patents, although PME lawsuits involved these patents to a much greater extent. Specifically, about 84 percent of PME lawsuits from 2007 to 2011 involved software-related patents, while about 35 percent of operating company lawsuits did. However, operating companies brought a greater number of lawsuits involving software-related patents, given that they filed more lawsuits overall.[42] By defendant, software-related patents were used to sue 93 percent of the defendants in PME suits and 46 percent of the defendants in operating company suits (see fig. 6).

Figure 6: Estimated Percentage of PME and Operating Company Lawsuits and Defendants Associated with Software-Related Patents, 2007 to 2011

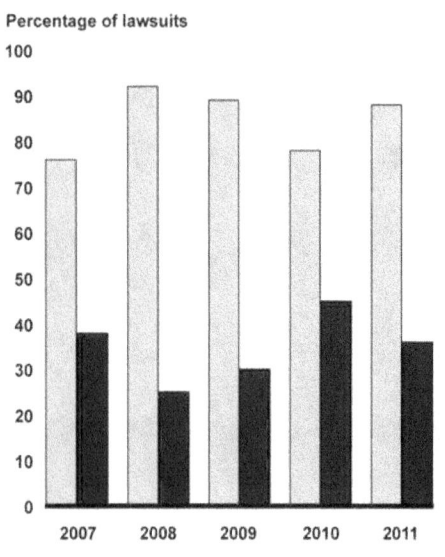
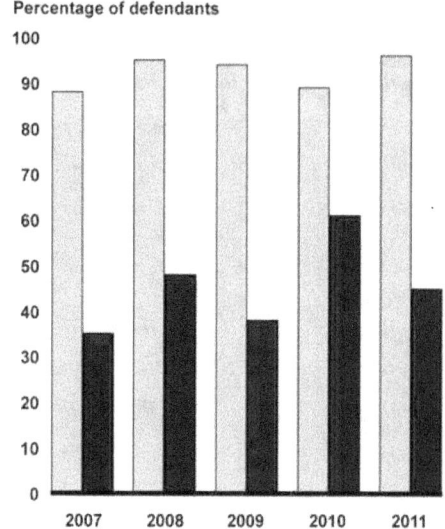

Source: GAO analysis of Lex Machina data.

Note: Percentage of lawsuit and defendant estimates are subject to a margin of error of up to plus or minus 10 percentage points. Software-related patents include a number of patent classes that are most likely to include patents with software-related claims, and this includes business method patents. PMEs focus solely on asserting typically purchased patents.

Technology-related operating companies were not the only companies sued for infringing software-related patents; other sectors were also sued

---

[42]We estimate that, from 2007 to 2011, operating companies and related entities brought 3,037 lawsuits involving software-related patents, while PMEs and likely PMEs brought 2,093 such lawsuits.

GAO-13-465 Patent Litigation

for infringing such patents, including retail companies and local governments. We estimate that 39 percent of suits involving software-related patents were against firms in nontechnology sectors, according to our analysis of 2007 to 2011 data. One representative from a retail company noted that historically, all of the patent infringement lawsuits brought against the company used to be related to products they sold. However, as of mid-2012, the representative said that half of the lawsuits against the company were related to e-commerce software that the company uses for its shopping website—such as software that allows customers to locate their stores on the website—and were brought by PMEs. Representatives of retail and pharmaceutical companies told us they also defend lawsuits brought by PMEs related to features on their websites—typically software that outside vendors provide to them, rather than something they developed. Additionally, city public transit agencies have been sued for allegedly infringing patents by using software for real-time public transit arrival notifications, according to a few stakeholders we interviewed.

Common Venues of Recent Patent Litigation

For 2007 to 2011, an estimated 32 percent of patent infringement lawsuits were filed in 3 of the 94 federal district courts: the Eastern District of Texas, the District of Delaware, and the Central District of California. These districts also had the most lawsuits filed for the period of 2000 to 2011 (see fig. 7).

Figure 7: Distribution of Total Patent Infringement Lawsuits across U.S. District Courts from 2000 to 2011

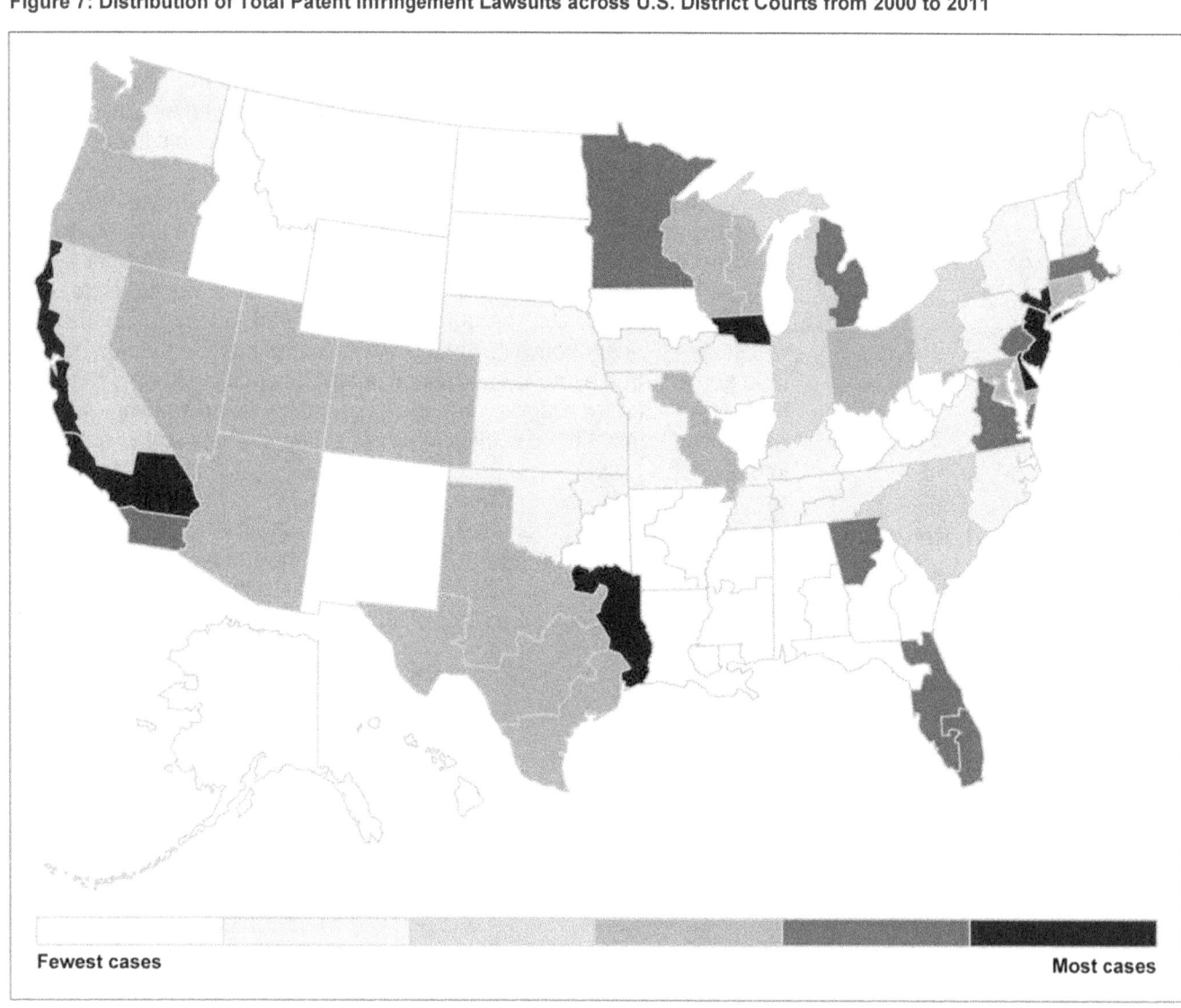

Fewest cases

Most cases

Sources: GAO analysis of Lex Machina data; Map Resources (map)

In addition, our review of 2007 to 2011 litigation data shows that PMEs filed more lawsuits in the Eastern District of Texas than other types of plaintiffs. Specifically, from 2007 to 2011, 39 percent of PME and likely PME lawsuits were filed in the Eastern District of Texas, compared to about 8 percent of lawsuits filed by all other plaintiffs. Some stakeholders we interviewed said that in their view this occurs because juries in this district favor patent owners over alleged infringers.[43] In addition, one study we reviewed that looked at all decisions for all patent lawsuits from 1995 to 2011, showed that the Eastern District of Texas, the Eastern District of Virginia, and the District of Delaware were among the top districts for quicker trials, higher success rates, and higher damage awards for patent owners.[44]

Outcomes and Costs of Recent Patent Litigation

An estimated 21 percent of patent infringement cases from 2007 to 2011 were still ongoing. Of the remaining cases, our analysis shows that about 86 percent either ended or likely ended in a settlement. This occurred because both parties agreed to a judgment that the judge sanctioned, both parties agreed to end the lawsuit, or the plaintiff, who had brought the lawsuit, asked for it to be dismissed.[45] Lawsuits brought by both operating companies and PMEs settled or likely settled at similar rates.[46] Less than 3 percent of the cases that were not ongoing ended in a trial and judgment, or were on appeal, which was consistent with what some representatives of operating companies told us—very few of their lawsuits go to trial because they settle quickly to avoid high litigation costs.

We were not able to determine litigation cost information from our sample data, and we found very little information on the costs of patent

---

[43]Defendants can request that the district court transfer the case to another court in certain circumstances. If the district court denies the defendant's request, the defendant can ask the Federal Circuit to order the district court to transfer the lawsuit. For example, in 2008, the Federal Circuit ordered the Eastern District of Texas to transfer a case because none of the parties had an office and no witnesses or evidence were located in the district. *In re: TS Tech*, 551 F.3d 1315 (Fed. Cir. 2008). According to one legal commentator, the precedent in this case and other Federal Circuit transfers likely resulted in fewer lawsuits being filed in the Eastern District of Texas.

[44]PricewaterhouseCoopers, *2012 Patent Litigation Study: Litigation continues to rise amid growing awareness of patent value. www.pwc.com/us/en/forensic-services/publications/2012-patent-litigation-study.jhtml.* Pricewaterhouse looked at decisions identified through the WestLaw database.

[45]We estimate that 46 percent of all patent infringement lawsuits filed between 2007 and 2011 ended or likely ended in a settlement within 1 year of being filed.

[46]Of the lawsuits that were not ongoing, 86 percent of PME suits and 87 percent of operating company suits settled, which was not a statistically significant difference. However, our analysis showed a statistically significant difference between suits involving software-related patents, of which 82 percent settled compared with 89 percent of suits that did not involve software-related patents.

infringement lawsuits in court records. Further, as one stakeholder we interviewed noted, all litigation is expensive, not just patent infringement litigation. According to a 2011 nongeneralizable survey of patent lawyers by AIPLA, the cost of defending one patent infringement lawsuit, which excludes any damages awarded, was from $650,000 to $5 million in 2011, depending on how much was at risk.[47] As for damages awarded, a 2012 study that looked at all district court patent decisions that proceeded through trial from 1995 to 2011 found that the median damage award was over $5 million dollars and that damage awards in NPE cases were higher than in other types of suits.[48] The authors of a 2012 paper who collected data from a nonrandom, nongeneralizable set of 82 operating companies noted that total litigation costs for NPE suits, including damages awarded and legal fees, were around $300,000 for small and medium companies and $600,000 for large companies.[49] The author of another 2012 paper sought to examine the impacts of NPE litigation on small companies and collected data from a nonrandom, nongeneralizable set of 223 small technology companies.[50] Of the 79 companies that indicated that they had received a patent demand, 31 reported that the demand affected the company in various ways, including reduced hiring or a reduced value of their company—which the author collectively described as "significant operational impacts."

| Stakeholders Reported That Patent Assertion Occurs Without Firms Ever Filing Lawsuits | In addition to lawsuits, patent assertion occurs without firms ever filing lawsuits, but the extent of this practice is unclear because we were not able to find reliable data on patent assertion outside of the court system. According to representatives of some operating companies we spoke with, they often get letters from patent owners offering licenses for the |

---

[47]For the 18 percent of those lawyers that responded, AIPLA reports that the median legal cost for one patent infringement lawsuit was $650,000 when less than $1 million was at risk for damages; $2.5 million when between $1 million and $25 million was at risk for damages; and $5 million when more than $25 million was at risk for damages. These costs include legal fees and exclude damage awards.

[48]PricewaterhouseCoopers, *2012 Patent Litigation Study: Litigation continues to rise amid growing awareness of patent value.* Pricewaterhouse looked at decisions identified through the WestLaw database.

[49]James E. Bessen and Michael J. Meurer, *The Direct Costs from NPE Disputes,* Law and Economics Research Paper No. 12-34 (Boston University School of Law: June 28, 2012).

[50]Colleen Chien, *Startups and Patent Trolls,* Santa Clara Univ. Legal Studies Research Paper No. 09-12 (Sept. 28, 2012).

use of their patents. They said that these letters, which they refer to as "demand letters," sometimes threaten lawsuits if the parties do not reach a licensing agreement. These company representatives told us that for every patent infringement lawsuit filed against them, they might receive many times more letters notifying them of potential infringement and offering licenses.[51] Representatives from a few operating companies we spoke with said that these letters can sometimes help to resolve issues without litigation, but that at times the letters can be so vague that they do not reference the patents at issue or what products the operating company sells that may be infringing these patents.

However, a few PME representatives told us that operating companies generally ignore their letters, thus leading the PMEs to sue the companies first to get their attention. A few of these PMEs also told us that they are more likely to sue without sending a demand letter after a 2007 Supreme Court decision expanded accused infringers' ability to file preemptive declaratory judgment lawsuits seeking determinations that the patent is invalid, unenforceable, or not being infringed.[52] The threat of a declaratory judgment lawsuit can derail patent owners' attempts to reach a licensing agreement, according to a few PMEs we spoke with.

Because licenses or payments resulting from out-of-court patent assertions are almost always confidential, it is difficult to know the cost of these settlements. The authors of the 2012 study noted above of a nonrandom, nongeneralizable set of 82 operating companies attempted to identify this cost. The 46 companies that provided data on costs reported that they spent an average of about $30 million on NPE suits, including both legal fees and settlements, which were settled without litigation from 2005 to 2011.

---

[51]The author of a 2012 study of a nonrandom, nongeneralizable set of 223 small technology companies noted above found that about two-thirds of the 79 companies that reported that they had received a demand from an NPE were not sued.

[52]*MedImmune Inc. v. Genentech*, 549 U.S. 118 (2007).

Stakeholders Identified Three Key Factors Contributing to Many Recent Patent Infringement Lawsuits

Stakeholders we spoke with identified three key factors that likely contributed to many recent patent infringement lawsuits: (1) unclear and overly broad patents, (2) the potential for disproportionately large damage awards, and (3) the increasing recognition that patents are a valuable asset.

Stakeholders Said That Some Patents Have Unclear Property Rights and Make Overly Broad Claims

Several of the stakeholders we spoke with, including representatives from PMEs, operating companies, and legal commentators, said that many recent patent infringement lawsuits are related to the prevalence of low-quality patents; that is, patents with unclear property rights, overly broad claims, or both. Although there is some inherent uncertainty associated with all patent claims, several of the stakeholders with this opinion noted that claims in software-related patents are often overly broad, unclear or both. Unclear and overly broad patents do not provide notice about their boundaries and the uncertainty of a patent's scope then usually needs to be resolved in court, according to some stakeholders we spoke with.

Stakeholders we interviewed identified several reasons why patents may be overly broad, unclear, or vague:

- Some stakeholders representing different interests, including operating companies, PMEs, and legal commentators, said the use of unclear terminology in patents can lead to a lack of understanding of patent claims and, therefore, what constitutes infringement, which needs to be resolved in court. For example, two of these stakeholders said the computer software industry does not have clear terminology or common vocabularies for describing concepts, innovations, and ideas. Language describing emerging technologies, such as software, may be inherently imprecise because these technologies are constantly evolving. In contrast, pharmaceutical drug patents are relatively clear because they use standardized scientific terminology, according to a few stakeholders.
- Some stakeholders, including operating companies and legal commentators, emphasized that claims in software patents sometimes define the scope of the invention by encompassing an

entire function—like sending an e-mail—rather than the specific means of performing that function.[53] According to a few stakeholders we spoke with, functional claims and other overly broad claims may allow patent owners who sue for infringement to argue in court that their patent covers (1) an entire technology when it may only cover a small improvement, or (2) future technologies that their patent did not originally intend to cover. For example, representatives from one PME we spoke with said they had successfully sued companies for infringement even though the companies were implementing their idea in a completely different manner than described in their patent—noting that they had patented their invention before the technology to best implement it was actually available. In addition, a few stakeholders noted that in certain circumstances patent owners can file a reissue application with PTO, which can sometimes broaden the scope of patents after they are issued.[54] In addition, a few stakeholders noted that patent owners can also file continuation applications during patent examination, which, depending on the type filed, allow new subject matter to be added to the patent application.[55]

• According to some stakeholders—including PMEs and representatives of operating companies that were sued for patent infringement—broad patents on concepts they would not expect to be patented make it easy to infringe a patent without intending to do so, although this is not a defense since patent infringement is a strict

---

[53]In addition, FTC recently reported that reliance on describing what an invention does rather than how it is created contributes to overly broad patents and a 2012 study also supports that view. U.S. Federal Trade Commission, *The Evolving IP Marketplace: Aligning Patent Notice and Remedies with Competition* (Washington, D.C.: March 2011). Mark A. Lemley, *Software Patents and the Return of Functional Claiming* (Stanford University, 2012).

[54]Applications for reissuance of defective patents—those which, through error, are deemed wholly or partly inoperative or invalid by reason of a defective specification or drawing or by reason of the patentee claiming more or less than he or she had a right to claim in the patent—cannot introduce new matter and must be filed within 2 years of the patent issuance if the reissued patent enlarges the scope of the original patent's claims.

[55]PTO recognizes three types of continuations and only one type allows the patent owner to claim subject matter not previously disclosed in the application. One patent owner told us he filed a continuation so that his patent would closely match software that was already being used but that his original application did not anticipate; he later won large settlements from the allegedly infringing companies.

liability offense.[56] For example, the software start-up and venture capital firms we spoke with said that many software-related patents they encountered were for obvious concepts and did not represent any real contribution to new technology. Other stakeholders, including operating companies, judges, and legal commentators, also said some patents, particularly software-related patents, should never have been issued because they were obvious, not novel, or lacked definiteness.

Unclear boundaries make it hard to determine whether a patent is actually related to a particular technology. Several diverse stakeholders, including PMEs, operating companies, legal commentators, and judges we interviewed said that many overly broad or vague patent claims do not sufficiently identify the scope of the patent's coverage. This lack of notice makes it difficult for entities to identify relevant existing patents and prior art before developing new products, according to some legal commentators and operating companies. This difficulty reduces the effectiveness of searching for existing patents to ensure the product being developed does not infringe on valid patents and, according to several stakeholders, including PMEs, legal commentators, and venture capital and start-up firms, entities do not always conduct patent searches. For example, representatives from a software start-up company we spoke with told us that searching for relevant patents before developing new products is unrealistic and diverts already scarce resources, particularly because their product development process can be as short as 2 months. In contrast, pharmaceutical company representatives we spoke with said that development of new drugs is so expensive that patent searches are a necessity and that they can conduct thorough searches because their patents are described clearly and are easy to find in industry databases.

In addition, a few stakeholders we spoke with told us that the sheer volume of patents makes searching for relevant patents before developing new products particularly difficult, especially for products that combine many patented technologies. For example, these stakeholders

---

[56]One study we reviewed looked at a sample of 193 complaints from two federal courts districts, the District of Delaware and the Eastern District of Texas, and found that allegations of copying occurred in 21 of the 193 complaints. The authors suggested this means that most accused infringers came up with the idea independently; however, as noted, patent infringement liability does not require proof of copying so patent owners do not need to allege it. Christopher A. Cotropia and Mark A. Lemley, *Copying in Patent Law*, 87 N.C.L. Rev. 1421 (2009).

we spoke with estimated that a typical smartphone uses from 50,000 to 250,000 patented technologies because such devices incorporate technologies from digital cameras, global positioning systems, and wireless communication. In contrast, pharmaceutical company representatives we spoke with said they are able to conduct thorough patent searches, in part, because there are fewer patents per drug. Determining the licenses a new product needs can be costly when many patents are involved; according to data from the AIPLA survey, the median cost for a legal validity and infringement opinion is $15,000 per patent.[57] Additionally, a technology start-up company told us that they may avoid patent searches because damage awards can be tripled for willful infringement, and by not searching for existing patents, they can claim ignorance.

Even if an entity conducts a patent search, identifies a relevant patent, and wants to avoid infringing it by obtaining a license to use it, according to several diverse stakeholders we spoke with, including PMEs, legal commentators, and operating companies, identifying the owner could be difficult because patent owners are not required to notify PTO of changes in assignment or ownership. According to some stakeholders we spoke with, finding patent owners is further complicated by the fact that some of these patent owners create subsidiary companies solely to hold their patent rights. In fact, several stakeholders we interviewed, including legal commentators, operating companies, and a PME, said that some entities intentionally hide the existence of their patents until a sector or company are using the patented invention without authorization and can be sued for infringement. Further, some economic literature we reviewed suggests that the numerous technologies in many products are sometimes patented by many different patent owners and can have overlapping rights, making it difficult and costly to determine which patents the operating company needs to license. We discuss PTO's current efforts to address these notice problems later in the report.

Most of the representatives from operating companies we interviewed said that PMEs specifically have played a role in the rise in patent infringement litigation. Some of the representatives from operating

---

[57]AIPLA, *Report of the Economic Survey 2011* (Arlington, Va.: July 2011). Entities can seek patent validity and infringement opinions on patents found during a patent search. A patent validity opinion is a legal opinion as to whether a patent is valid and a patent infringement opinion is a legal opinion as to whether a product infringes a patent.

companies also said that PMEs are often more willing to bring lawsuits based on a broad interpretation of their patents' claims because they cannot be countersued for patent infringement since they do not produce a product. Some economic literature we reviewed suggests that accused infringers have an incentive to settle quickly to avoid the uncertainty of claim construction and high litigation costs, particularly if they face very high costs of changing their products to avoid infringement.[58] Although a few stakeholders said that operating companies have also brought lawsuits alleging infringement of poor quality patents that they do not practice, and several stakeholders, including PMEs, operating companies, and legal commentators, said they believe the prevalence of low quality patents was driving recent increases in litigation more than PME suits.[59]

Stakeholders Believe the Potential for Disproportionately Large Damage Awards from the Courts Can Incentivize Litigation

Disproportionately large damages awarded by the courts can motivate patent owners to file lawsuits, according to several stakeholders, we spoke with, including operating companies, PMEs, and legal commentators. According to some stakeholders, the potential for large damage awards may encourage some patent owners to file lawsuits in the hope that the accused infringer settles to avoid going to court. A few representatives of operating companies told us that companies prefer to settle lawsuits before trial for smaller amounts of money rather than risk having to pay large damage awards and legal fees, even if they know the case against them is weak. They said that some patent owners file infringement lawsuits knowing that defendants will settle the case before the court determines whether infringement occurred or the patents are valid. In addition, some operating company representatives said that patent owners often sue operating companies that have purchased licenses to use software in order to get settlements from numerous infringers rather than suing the vendor. One PME we spoke with said that although it tries to sue technology vendors whenever possible, it sues end

---

[58]This practice imposes social costs to businesses that are sued in this manner, according to economists. We were not able to identify suits associated with overly broad patents in our analysis of Lex Machina data, or the extent to which overly broad patents were associated with PME lawsuits, and were not able to estimate the overall economic social costs of this type of patent infringement litigation.

[59]As noted earlier, our analysis of litigation data showed that PME suits accounted for about half of the increase in defendants between 2007 and 2011, while suits involving software-related patents accounted for around 89 percent of the increase in defendants.

users most of the time because these are usually profitable companies, and there is greater potential for larger settlements.

Until 2011, damage awards could be calculated using the 25 percent rule—whereby the alleged infringer would pay a royalty rate equivalent to 25 percent of the expected profits for the product that incorporates the patent at issue. As a result, according to some stakeholders, damage awards were outsized and did not reflect the value of the patent or the patent's contribution to the product at issue, making it possible for the owner of only a few patents to capture most of the profit from a product, even though thousands of other patents also contributed to the development of the product. In a 2011 report, FTC noted that some legal rules for calculating damages were not grounded in economic analysis and therefore may under- or overcompensate patent owners for infringement in comparison to the market.[60] FTC reported that overcompensation can overincentivize patenting and patent litigation. Moreover, the FTC report included concerns from some industry participants that the value added by one patented technology may be very small relative to the price of the entire product for complex products.

In its 2011 report, FTC made a number of recommendations to courts, including that damage awards—since they are based on reasonable royalties—should not be higher than the incremental value of the patented invention over the next best alternative and should not be punitive. Some stakeholders noted that changes to damage awards occurred after a 2011 Federal Circuit decision eliminated the use of the 25 percent rule because it was fundamentally flawed and established a rule of apportionment whereby damages are apportioned according to the patent at issue's contribution to the product.[61] These stakeholders noted this 2011 decision and other decisions have had the effect of lowering damage awards to reflect a patent's value or eliminated the potential for

---

[60]U.S. Federal Trade Commission, *The Evolving IP Marketplace: Aligning Patent Notice and Remedies with Competition* (Washington, D.C.: March 2011).

[61]*Uniloc USA, Inc., v. Microsoft Corp.*, 632 F.3d 1292 (Fed. Cir. 2011).

enhanced damages.[62] Despite some of this progress, a few stakeholders noted that there is still a need for improvement in the way damages are calculated.

Stakeholders Noted the Recognition of Patents as a Valuable Asset May Have Contributed to Recent Patent Issuance and Litigation

Several stakeholders, including PMEs and legal commentators, we interviewed said that the recognition that patents are a more valuable asset than once assumed may have contributed to recent patent issuance trends and patent infringement lawsuits. Within the last 10 years, technology companies in particular have increasingly realized that patents are valuable and can be important to their corporate strategy, according to some of these stakeholders. This trend may have started, according to literature we reviewed, when Texas Instruments Inc. was looking for additional sources of revenue in the 1980s and started to more aggressively assert its patents to increase revenue.[63] Prior to this, entities used patents to protect inventions rather than to generate revenue, according to some stakeholders, including legal commentators and a PME, we spoke with.

Despite the new value placed on patents, some industries may have slightly different approaches to patenting. For example, a few representatives of venture capital and software start-up firms told us that they do not always apply for patents until their companies are well established because patent attorneys are expensive, and the process is

---

[62] Enhanced damages can be awarded for willful infringement but some stakeholders said that recent Federal Circuit decisions made it harder to prove willful infringement and obtain enhanced damages. *Knorr-Bremse Systeme Fuer Nutzfahrzeuge GmbH v. Dana*, 383 F.3d 1337 (Fed. Cir. 2004) (alleged patent infringers who invoke attorney-client privilege or work product protection over advice of counsel regarding whether its activities would be an infringement of a valid patent does not give rise to an adverse interference and failure to obtain legal advice does not give rise to an adverse inference with respect to willful infringement); *In re: Seagate Technology*, 497 F.3d 1360 (Fed. Cir. 2007) (proof of willful infringement permitting enhanced damages requires the patent owner (1) to show by clear and convincing evidence that the infringer acted despite an objectively high likelihood that its actions constituted infringement of a valid patent and (2) demonstrate that this objectively-defined risk was either known to the accused infringer or so obvious that it should have been known but there is no affirmative obligation to obtain opinion of counsel).

[63] See Colleen V. Chien, *From Arms Race to Marketplace: The Complex Patent Ecosystem and Its Implications for the Patent System*, 62 Hastings L.J. 297 (2010); Kevin Rivette and David Kline, Rembrandts in the Attic: Unlocking the Hidden Value of Patents, (Boston, Ma.: Harvard Business School Press, 2000).

time consuming. They told us that the cost of R&D is low relative to the cost of applying for a patent, so there is minimal incentive in the software industry to patent in order to recoup R&D costs. For example, representatives from one small software company we spoke with said that they could develop a product in a little as 2 months with only a few programmers. They also noted that it is relatively easy to get patents on their software even with their minimal R&D efforts—it is just a matter of paying the patent attorney's fees. On the other hand, several representatives from the pharmaceutical industry told us that patents are actually critical to their ability to recoup the costs of developing a new drug, which can cost as much as $1 billion and take from 10 to 15 years.

Further, several stakeholders, including operating companies, PMEs, and legal commentators, we interviewed said that investors have played a role in the increasing number of patent infringement lawsuits. Specifically, according to some of these stakeholders, some PMEs have financial backers who fund the purchase and enforcement of patents and expect to see a return on their investment, sometimes turning to contingency fee law firms to carry out the lawsuits, where the law firm pays all of the litigation costs but shares in any award or settlement.[64]

Furthermore, economic literature suggests that inventors who do not have the resources or skills to enforce patents on their own benefit from partnering with PMEs that specialize in patent monetization, and this was confirmed by some of the stakeholders we spoke with. For example, one inventor we spoke with said that he was able to sell his patents to a PME that specialized in patent litigation when his start-up company failed, which allowed him to fund a new company. Representatives from a university we spoke with also said universities look to outside entities, such as PMEs, to finance patent infringement litigation because universities cannot cover the up-front costs of filing a lawsuit. Representatives from one PME we spoke with said that they helped a small inventor get the attention of large technology companies that were infringing his patent and ignoring his licensing requests. In addition, one

---

[64]For example, one PME we spoke with said its business model was to value patents based on legal, financial, and technical factors and then either (1) offer an inventor no up-front payment but a large cut of a settlement with accused infringers, (2) offer the inventor a small payment up front and a medium-sized portion of the settlement, or (3) pay the inventor up front and retain all of the settlement. One legal commentator, however, noted that contingency fee lawsuits are not unique to patent infringement litigation.

patent broker we spoke with said that well-known operating companies often do not want to file patent infringement suits because of potential public backlash, so they sell or transfer their patents but retain an interest in any settlement or award.

New Initiatives in the Courts May Affect Patent Litigation

The federal court system is implementing some new initiatives to improve the handling of patent cases. A pilot program was established for certain U.S. district courts to encourage the enhancement of expertise in patent cases among district court judges and a model order was issued in response to high discovery costs for e-mails and other electronic documents in patent cases—known as e-discovery. In addition, some recent decisions in the Federal Circuit and the Supreme Court may also affect future patent infringement litigation.

Efforts to Improve Courts' Handling of Patent Cases

In January 2011, Congress established a pilot program in certain U.S. district courts to encourage the enhancement of expertise in patent cases among district court judges.[65] This pilot program would create a cadre of judges who have advanced knowledge of patents due to more intensified experience in handling the cases, according to a statement made during the congressional debate for the law. Specifically, the law required AOUSC to designate at least 6 district courts that met certain eligibility requirements to participate in a 10-year pilot program.[66] As of December 2012, AOUSC had designated all 14 federal district courts that applied as participants. Currently, 7 of the 14 district courts participating in the pilot program have adopted case management rules to govern patent cases, such as how cases are allocated to judges in the program, although some districts' rules predated the program.[67]

---

[65]Pub. L. No. 111-349 (2011).

[66]To be eligible for designation, district courts had to: (1) be among the 15 district courts in which the largest number of patent cases were filed in 2010; or (2) have adopted, or intend to adopt, local rules for patent cases.

[67]The law requires patent cases to be randomly assigned to judges in districts participating in the pilot program regardless of whether they are designated by the court's chief judge to hear patent cases. Nondesignated judges may decline to accept the case, which would then be randomly assigned to one of the designated judges.

Some legal commentators and other stakeholders we interviewed said they were hopeful that the pilot program would lead to some meaningful improvements in patent case management in the courts. However, a few judges we interviewed said that more resources are needed to improve the handling of patent cases and that the needed resources were not appropriated to implement the pilot program.[68] For example, they told us that hiring additional law clerks would help with the increased workload and processing of patent cases resulting from participation in the pilot program. Because participation in the pilot program does not come with additional resources, some districts decided not to participate, according to the judges we spoke with. For example, a district court judge told us that his district court did not volunteer for the pilot program because funds were not appropriated to implement it. In general, several stakeholders we spoke with agreed that it is too early to tell what impact the patent pilot project will ultimately have on patent litigation.

Efforts to Reduce Discovery Costs

In response to high discovery costs, in September 2011, the Advisory Council for the U.S. Court of Appeals for the Federal Circuit issued a model order regarding discovery for e-mail and other electronic documents (known as e-discovery) targeted to patent cases.[69] According to some legal commentators and judges we interviewed, the technical complexity of patent cases leads to expansive discovery requests that are time consuming and expensive and, as is typically the case with most documents produced in discovery, do not necessarily produce documents used at trial. For example, a study conducted by AIPLA found that discovery costs can range from $350,000 to $3 million, depending on the size of the potential settlement.[70] One judge we spoke to said that only a few of the documents in discovery are actually used at trial—often less

---

[68]The law also requires AOUSC to keep certain congressional committees informed on a periodic basis while the pilot project is in effect and to submit a report to those committees in 2016 and 2021.

[69]The Advisory Council was established to review, study, and make recommendations on the rules of practice and internal operating procedures of the court. The Chief Judge of the court unveiled the model order at a meeting of the Federal Circuit Bar Association and the Eastern District of Texas Bar Association. The model order is a template, or model, for judges to adopt and issue in patent infringement lawsuits.

[70]AIPLA, *Report of the Economic Survey 2011* (Arlington, Va.: July 2011). The estimated cost of litigation through discovery was $350,000 when the damage stakes are less than $1 million, $1.5 million when the stakes are between $1 million and $25 million, and $3 million when the stakes are over $25 million.

than one document in 10,000—and representatives from one operating company told us that about 2,000 of the 10 million documents they were asked to produce were actually used in a recent trial.

After the issuance of the e-discovery model order, a few federal district courts have adopted similar rules to streamline e-discovery in patent cases, according to legal commentators we spoke with. Courts with e-discovery rules are more efficient and reduce litigation costs for everyone involved, according to a few judges we spoke with. For example, under the model order, discovery begins with an exchange of core documentation concerning the patent, allegedly infringing product, prior art, and finances before an exchange of e-mails.[71] However, at least one federal district court that handles a large volume of patent infringement cases declined to adopt specific discovery rules, noting that it would be a mistake for the courts to bind themselves to specific rules given differences among cases.

In general, several stakeholders we spoke with agreed that it is too early to tell what impact e-discovery rules will ultimately have on patent litigation.

Evolving Case Law

Several federal judges and other stakeholders we interviewed said that the judiciary had the ability to address some of the aforementioned factors contributing to patent infringement litigation in court decisions and that certain recent court decisions have helped to address some of these problems. In the future, they said the courts would continue working to address them. Specifically, these stakeholders said that recent court decisions about what constitutes patentable subject matter and what satisfies the obviousness and definiteness requirements would help combat overly broad and ill-defined patent claims once the decisions were incorporated into PTO's patent examination guidelines and implemented by examiners. For example, two stakeholders said that a 2012 Supreme Court decision restricted what constitutes a patentable process and a 2007 Supreme Court decision made it easier to combine separate pieces of prior art to prove a patented invention was obvious

---

[71]The model order presumptively limits the number of each party's e-mail requests, but the parties may jointly agree to modify the limits or request court modification for good cause.

and, thus, not eligible for a patent.[72] In addition, as we discussed earlier, some stakeholders also identified several decisions that have changed damages law. Despite these cases, some stakeholders said that the judicial system has contributed to recent problems in patent infringement litigation and is either unable or unwilling to rectify them. For example, they noted that judges should be more willing to award attorney fees in exceptional cases to the winning party in order to address the growing number of patent infringement lawsuits.

PTO Has Taken Actions to Improve Patent Quality and Implement New AIA Proceedings That May Affect Patent Litigation in the Future

PTO has taken several recent actions that are likely to affect patent quality and patent litigation in the future, including agency initiatives and changes required by AIA. For example, PTO is implementing initiatives to continue to improve the quality of software-related patents and to improve patent examination searches. The agency is also implementing the new administrative trial proceedings created by AIA.

PTO Is Implementing Initiatives to Address Problems with Unclear Patents and Patent Search

We identified four initiatives that PTO is currently undertaking to address patent quality and patent search:

- In February 2011, PTO issued supplemental guidelines to assist in the examination of claims in applications for compliance with the definiteness requirement and began training patent examiners in how to implement them. PTO often updates its patent examination manual or issues guidance to patent examiners in response to changes in case law and these recently issued supplemental guidelines try to ensure that all technologies receive consistent examination practices, according to PTO officials. These guidelines specifically address examination of claims with functional language—which recites a feature by what it does rather than by what it is—in computer-implemented claims. For example, the guidelines state that examiners

---

[72] *Mayo Collaborative Servs. v. Prometheus Labs*, _ U.S. _, 132 S. Ct. 1289 (2012); *KSR International Co. v. Teleflex, Inc.*, 550 U.S. 398 (2007).

should determine whether the application discloses the computer and algorithm that perform the claimed function in sufficient detail that someone of ordinary skill in the art would know how to program the computer to perform the claimed function, and that the inventor was in possession of the claimed invention. The guidelines further noted that the algorithm may be expressed in any understandable terms and generally do not call for the application to contain actual computer code. The supplemental guidelines attempt to make examination of applications consistent and resulting patents clearer across all technologies, according to PTO officials. In May 2012, an internal PTO review showed that PTO examiners were making 4 to 6 percent more rejections in patent applications across all technology areas based on claims not being clear and definite than before the supplemental guidelines were issued. PTO officials said patent requirements are established by statute and case law, which constrains the agency's ability to alter requirements for patent applications. PTO officials told us that only court decisions or statutory changes could change the law to require more detail for algorithms in software-related patents, for example.

- In November 2011, in response to the recommendations from FTC's 2011 report, PTO acknowledged that more uniform terminology would help to improve the quality of software-related patents and began working to establish a partnership with the software industry to address this issue.[73] In January 2013, PTO announced the Software Partnership—a cooperative effort with the software industry to explore ways to enhance the quality of software-related patents, including through the use of more uniform terminology. Subsequently, roundtable meetings with the software industry were held in New York City, New York and Stanford, California in February 2013.[74]

- Additionally, PTO is working to implement a new patent classification system, called the Cooperative Patent Classification (CPC), which launched in January 2013. Since October 2010, PTO and the European Patent Office (EPO) have been collaborating to develop the CPC, which is a joint patent classification system that is intended to allow companies and patent applicants to conduct more effective

---

[73]U.S. Federal Trade Commission, *The Evolving IP Marketplace: Aligning Patent Notice and Remedies with Competition* (Washington, D.C.: March 2011), (FTC Report Recommends Improvements in Patent System to Promote Innovation and Benefit Consumers).

[74]PTO announced these public meetings by public notice. 78 Fed. Reg. 292 (Jan. 3, 2013).

searches for patents that might be related to technologies they are developing or planning to use, which may reduce some of the infringement that contributes to current patent litigation, according to documents we reviewed. CPC is also designed to allow for more frequent updating of patent classes, so that similar technologies can be grouped together, which should improve PTO's ability to adapt to emerging technologies quickly, according to agency documents we reviewed.

- PTO is also working to provide greater transparency on patent ownership by and issued a notice in November 2012 to obtain public input on regulations it was considering to require patent ownership information to be verified and updated at certain times during patent examination and after patent issuance. Specifically, PTO is currently considering issuing regulations that would require ownership information to be verified and updated periodically. In addition, PTO held a round table discussion in January 2013 to obtain public input on how the agency could collect and provide such information to the public. Since holding the round table, PTO officials have been considering the input and written comments and have been discussing what the appropriate next steps should be. PTO officials noted, however, that the agency does not have substantive rulemaking authority so its ability to issue regulations requiring updates to the ownership information is limited without additional statutory authority.

In addition to these initiatives, in 2009 PTO began a patent quality initiative to measure and improve overall patent quality. After public comment and round table discussions, PTO released a set of new metrics in 2010 for fiscal year 2011 to assess patent quality throughout examination, rather than solely at the end of examination, which had been its practice. These metrics include, among other things, looking at the timeliness of patent examiners' decisions and whether examiners reject claims for the right reasons.[75] However, the agency generally does not review patent examination quality after patents are issued. PTO officials said that they did not examine the nature of patent infringement litigation and issues in dispute or review trends in such litigation. In 2003, the

---

[75]According to PTO, the new metrics expand the previous procedures for measuring examination quality and will reveal quality issues arising during the examination and identify their sources so that problems may be remediated by training. See the following for more information on PTO's patent quality metrics: http://www.uspto.gov/dashboards/patents/main.dashxml.

National Academies reported that litigation rates could be a useful measure of post-grant patent quality, presuming that litigated patents define less clear boundaries.[76] One study in the National Academies' report examined the link between examiner inputs, including the number of hours used to examine a patent, and the likelihood that the patent would end up in a lawsuit. The study found a statistically significant result, implying that patents that examiners spend more time examining are less likely to be involved in litigation, suggesting the patents are of higher quality.[77]

In February 2013, PTO officials said that they generally try to adapt to developments in patent law and industry to improve patent quality, as they are doing with their new examination guidelines and their software-related patent partnership. However, the agency does not currently use information on patent litigation in initiating actions like these. However, some staff in PTO's Office of the Chief Economist have suggested that analyzing relationships between the types of patents involved in infringement litigation and internal patent examination data, including the timeline between the filing and grant of a patent and changes in the wording of claims could potentially benefit patent quality and examination by identifying meaningful patterns in the examination of patents that end up in court.[78] As noted, our analysis of litigation data showed that about two-thirds of patent infringement defendants were sued for infringing software-related patents. Given the extent of litigation associated with these patents, examining trends in patent infringement litigation, including the types of patents and issues in dispute, and linking this information to internal data on patent examination, could provide PTO with information to improve patent quality and the examination process. However, PTO

---

[76]National Academy of Sciences, Committee on Intellectual Property Rights in the Knowledge-Based Economy, National Research Council, *Patents in the Knowledge-Based Economy,* Wesley M. Cohen and Stephen A. Merrill, eds. (Washington, D.C., National Academies Press, 2003).

[77]The results suggested that an additional hour of patent examination per application would be associated with a decrease in litigation by as many as 24 to 26 infringement complaints annually. The study, using data from 1996 and 1997, estimated that the savings associated with this reduction in suits would have been greater than the cost of the additional examiner hours.

[78]PTO's Office of the Chief Economist was created in 2010. See also J. Lanjouw. and M. Schankerman, *Characteristics of Patent Litigation: A Window on Competition,* The RAND Journal of Economics, vol. 32, no. 1 (Spring 2001), pp. 129-151.

staff economists said that looking at litigation trends was not without challenges. For example, they said that less than 2 percent of patents end up in court. In addition, patents usually end up in court long after they are issued, and examination procedures may have long since changed. PTO officials and a few stakeholders also noted that there are other factors that affect litigation trends, including economic conditions and inherent differences among industries.

PTO Is Implementing AIA Post-Grant Review Proceedings

PTO is in the process of implementing the three new post-grant review proceedings created by AIA and described previously—inter partes review, post-grant review, and a transitional program for covered business method patents. These proceedings replace or supplement certain reexamination proceedings conducted by patent examiners with proceedings conducted by judges at PTO's Patent Trial and Appeal Board—making them more closely resemble a patent trial, according to PTO officials we spoke with.[79] According to some stakeholders, these proceedings are most likely to be used by companies that have been sued for patent infringement. PTO issued rules to govern the proceedings in August 2012 and hired additional judges soon after AIA was passed. Specifically, PTO's Patent Trial and Appeal Board plans to move from 100 to more than 200 judges on staff by the end of 2013, according to PTO documents we reviewed. In addition, judges at the Board have been coordinating with stakeholders in the patent community to create a streamlined discovery process for these proceedings. The judges told us they want to avoid the massive discovery requests that add time and expense to patent trials in federal district courts, but said that details of how they handle discovery will continue to evolve over time.[80] The director of PTO is required to study and report to Congress on how these and other provisions of AIA are being implemented no later than September 16, 2015. According to agency officials, PTO plans to meet this 2015 deadline, and the agency has started collecting and publishing information on the number of times the new AIA proceedings are being

---

[79]Prior to AIA's provisions taking effect on September 16, 2012, patent reexamination proceedings consisted of:(1) inter partes reexamination conducted by patent examiners, which AIA replaced with inter partes review, a proceeding conducted by the Patent Trial and Appeal Board and (2) ex-parte reexamination.

[80]In addition, judges at the Board told us they are working with stakeholders in the patent community to balance some stakeholders' need for additional pages in their written submissions with the Board's need to complete the post-grant reviews in a timely way.

used and the timing of implementation. As of July 31st, 2013, there had been 395 requests for inter partes reviews and 39 requests for review under the transitional program for covered business method patents, according to data from PTO.

Given that challenging a patent's validity is a common defense for those who have been accused of patent infringement, PTO officials we spoke with mentioned that the new post-grant proceedings may have the potential to reduce future patent litigation because they offer a less costly and faster alternative to settling patent disputes in federal district courts. For example, a representative of a number of technology companies we spoke with estimated that the legal and filing fees for using one of these proceedings would be between $166,000 and $390,000, depending on the proceeding, for an average patent, while legal fees could be upwards of $5 million for an infringement case filed in district court. According to the Board judges we spoke with, these proceedings will be faster than most litigation in district court—which takes 2-½ years for the patent infringement trial to begin on average, according to a recent study—because the regulations stipulate that they normally are to conclude within 1 year of being initiated.[81] However, representatives from some operating companies said that they will not use these post-grant review proceedings if federal judges do not consistently delay the costly trials until the Board completes its review.[82] In the past, federal judges have not always been willing to suspend a lawsuit while waiting for PTO to conduct reexaminations, but may be more likely to do this given the regulatory 1 year timeline, according to these representatives. Judges at the Board told us they are working to ensure that the post-grant review proceedings are completed within 1 year. In addition, some operating company representatives we spoke with said that post-grant review in particular would be of limited utility since they only have 9 months after a patent is

---

[81]PricewaterhouseCoopers, *2012 Patent Litigation Study: Litigation continues to rise amid growing awareness of patent value.*

[82] Under AIA, if an entity submits a request for inter partes or post-grant review and then subsequently files a lawsuit, but not a counterclaim, challenging the validity of a patent claim in federal district court, the lawsuit is automatically suspended until certain events occur. In addition, AIA specifies factors judges are to consider in deciding whether to suspend a lawsuit alleging patent infringement at the request of a party because of a transitional covered business method patent proceeding. Requests for inter partes review and post-grant review cannot be granted if the requester (or real party in interest) previously filed a lawsuit challenging the validity of the patent's claims—but not a counterclaim—before the date on which the request is filed.

issued to file a request for review, but usually only learn about a patent's existence after being sued or receiving a demand letter, which is often many years after the patent has been issued.

Finally, representatives from some operating companies said they are not planning to use post-grant review to challenge a patent's validity because an adverse final decision by the Board generally prohibits them from challenging the patent's validity again in court.[83] These representatives said that they consider this to be a major flaw in post-grant review. However, a few other stakeholders said that patent owners need certainty in their patent's validity and that the same party should not be able to challenge the patent's validity through post-grant review and in the federal courts. Judges at the Board said they were aware of this issue and would continue to monitor it.

Conclusions

Public discussion surrounding patent infringement litigation often focuses on the increasing role of NPEs. However, our analysis indicates that regardless of the type of litigant, lawsuits involving software-related patents accounted for about 89 percent of the increase in defendants between 2007 and 2011, and most of the suits brought by PMEs involved software-related patents. This suggests that the focus on the identity of the litigant—rather than the type of patent—may be misplaced. PTO's recent efforts to work with the software industry to more uniformly define software terminology and make it easier to identify relevant patents and patent owners may strengthen the U.S. patent system. Further, PTO has available internal data on the patent examination process that could be linked to litigation data, and a 2003 National Academies study reported that using these types of data together could provide useful insights into patent quality. Examining the types of patents and issues in dispute represents a potentially valuable opportunity to improve the quality of issued patents and the patent examination process and to further strengthen the U.S. patent system.

---

[83]Specifically, parties who request post-grant or inter partes reviews that result in a final written decision may not assert in federal court or before ITC that a claim is invalid on any ground the party raised or reasonably could have raised during the review. Similarly, parties who receive a final written decision in a transitional program for covered business method patent proceedings are prohibited from subsequently asserting in federal court or before ITC that the claim is invalid on any ground that was raised during the proceeding.

Recommendation for Executive Action

We are recommending that the Secretary of Commerce direct the Director of PTO to consider examining trends in patent infringement litigation, including the types of patents and issues in dispute, and to consider linking this information to internal data on patent examination to improve the quality of issued patents and the patent examination process.

Agency Comments and Our Evaluation

We provided a copy of our draft report to PTO for review and comment. PTO concurred with key findings and our recommendation in its written comments, which are reproduced in appendix II. PTO also provided additional clarifying comments, which we incorporated as appropriate.

We are sending copies of this report to the Secretary of Commerce, the Federal Trade Commission, the International Trade Commission, the Administrative Office of the U.S. Courts, the appropriate congressional committees, and other interested parties. In addition, the report will be available at no charge on the GAO website at http://www.gao.gov.

If you or your staffs have any questions about this report, please contact me at (202) 512-3841 or ruscof@gao.gov. Contact points for our Offices of Congressional Relations and Public Affairs may be found on the last page of this report. GAO staff who made major contributions to this report are listed in appendix III.

Frank Rusco
Director, Natural Resources and Environment

The Honorable Patrick J. Leahy
Chairman
The Honorable Charles E. Grassley
Ranking Member
Committee on the Judiciary
United States Senate

The Honorable Bob Goodlatte
Chairman
The Honorable John Conyers, Jr.
Ranking Member
Committee on the Judiciary
House of Representatives

Appendix I: Objectives, Scope, and Methodology

Section 34 of the Leahy-Smith America Invents Act (AIA)[1] mandated that GAO conduct a study on the consequences of patent litigation by nonpracticing entities (NPE).[2] Our objectives were to determine: (1) what is known about the volume and characteristics of recent patent litigation activity; (2) what is known about the key factors that contribute to recent patent litigation trends; (3) what developments in the judicial system may affect patent litigation; and (4) what actions, if any, has the Patent and Trademark Office (PTO) recently taken that may affect patent litigation in the future.

To address all four of these objectives, we reviewed relevant laws, including AIA, and interviewed officials from PTO, the Federal Trade Commission (FTC), and the International Trade Commission (ITC). We also interviewed the following 44 stakeholders knowledgeable about patent litigation:

- Ten representatives from operating companies and industry groups from an array of industries, including software, computer hardware, retailers, and pharmaceuticals, who had been regularly sued in recent years for patent infringement. We identified these operating companies and industry groups by using patent infringement litigation data from 2005 through 2011, which we discuss below.
- Eight representatives of patent monetization entities (PME) and research firms that had regularly sued others in the past 10 years. We identified these PMEs by using patent infringement litigation data from 2005 through 2011, and they represent a range of business models.
- Fourteen legal commentators, economists, and consultants that had conducted research closely related to our objectives. We identified them through our review of academic literature on patent litigation and

---

[1]Pub. L. No.112-29 § 34 (2011).

[2]As noted in a September 7, 2011, letter from the Comptroller General to the chairs and ranking members of the congressional committees with jurisdiction over patents, the bill being considered at that time would have required a GAO study involving several questions for which reliable data were not available or which could not be obtained. The bill was enacted without change, but the Chair of the Senate Judiciary Committee, responding to these concerns, stated that GAO should note data and methodology limitations in its report prepared in response to the mandate. 157 CONG. REC. S 5402, S5441 (daily ed. Sept. 8, 2011) (statement of Sen. Leahy). Consequently, we developed report objectives consistent with these limitations, and we have noted specific data limitations throughout this report, as appropriate.

the patent system and they each had done work related to the issues we were asked to study.

- We also interviewed one representative each from two large research universities that license patents, two patent brokers who help others buy and sell patents, four venture capitalists, and four individual inventors at software start-up companies and at a small inventor advocacy group. We identified these universities, brokers, venture capitalists, and start-up companies based on our review of academic literature on patent litigation and the patent system and they were knowledgeable of the issues we were asked to study.

Because stakeholders varied in their expertise with various topics, not every stakeholder provided an opinion on every topic.

We were not able to find reliable data on patent assertion outside of the court system—which often consist of patent owners sending letters demanding licensing fees to potential infringers before filing suit and, as a result, our data analysis focuses on patent infringement litigation rather than patent assertion more broadly.

In addition to steps we took to address all four objectives, to describe what is known about the volume and characteristics of recent patent infringement litigation activity, we reported data from the American Intellectual Property Law Association's (AIPLA) 2011 survey on the costs of patent litigation.[3] We also reviewed academic literature on patent litigation and the patent system in general and assessed the methodology of the studies we reported on for soundness. To assess the reliability of data from PTO, AIPLA, and RPX, we conducted interviews and reviewed relevant methodology documentation. We found that these data were sufficiently reliable for purposes of this report.

We also analyzed patent infringement litigation data that we purchased from Lex Machina, a firm that collects and analyzes data on patent litigation.[4] Lex Machina maintains a database created from public

---

[3]AIPLA is a national, voluntary bar association constituted primarily of lawyers in private and corporate practice, in government service, and in the academic community. See AIPLA, *Report of the Economic Survey 2011* (Arlington, Va.: July 2011). AIPLA surveyed patent lawyers during 2011 and asked them to estimate legal costs for typical patent infringement cases. Their findings are based on an 18 percent response rate.

[4]We selected Lex Machina through a competitive contracting process to provide us patent infringement litigation data, select a sample of cases, and classify the plaintiffs in those cases.

electronic court filings for all patent infringement lawsuits filed in U.S. federal district courts, beginning in the year 2000. From this database, Lex Machina selected a random, generalizable sample of 100 lawsuits per year from 2007 through 2011, identifying for each lawsuit the patent(s) being litigated, the court hearing the lawsuit, and the lawsuit's outcome. The sample size allowed us to draw conclusions about patent infringement lawsuits filed in each of these years, with a margin of error of no more than plus or minus 5 percentage points over all these years and no more than plus or minus 10 percentage points for any particular year.[5] Each sample element was subsequently weighted in the analysis to account statistically for all the members of the population, including those that were not selected. To assess the reliability of data from Lex Machina, we met with Lex Machina staff, examined documentation, and tested and reviewed the sample data for completeness and accuracy. We found the data to be sufficiently reliable for our purposes. We also obtained patent infringement data from RPX, another firm that collects data on patent infringement lawsuits, in an effort to verify Lex Machina's litigant categorizations.[6]

---

[5]This sample allowed us to draw conclusions about the broader population of patent infringement lawsuits for each of these years and is therefore generalizable to all patent infringement lawsuits filed in federal district court from 2007 to 2011. However, as noted, estimates from the Lex Machina sample are subject to a 5 percent margin of error. This means that an estimate of 50 percent, for example, based on all years of data, would have a 95 percent confidence interval of between 45 percent and 55 percent. The margin of error is 10 percent when looking at individual years, which means that an estimate of 50 percent, for example, looking at an individual year, would have a 95 percent confidence interval of between 40 percent and 60 percent. Because Lex Machina followed a probability procedure based on random selections, the sample is only one of a large number of samples that might have been drawn. Since each sample could have provided different estimates, we express our confidence in the precision of our particular sample's results as a 95 percent confidence interval. This is the interval that would contain the actual population value for 95 percent of the samples that could have been drawn. Unless otherwise noted, the margin of error associated with the confidence intervals of our survey estimates is no more than plus or minus 10 percentage points at the 95 percent level of confidence.

[6]RPX also purchases patents itself, to prevent them from being asserted against its members. RPX provided us with summary data on the number of patent infringement lawsuits filed in federal district court since January 2005. RPX's data identified NPEs and other types of plaintiffs in these lawsuits by using a variety of factors, such as whether there was evidence that an entity sells or develops products. RPX representatives said that they used professional judgment to some extent in making these determinations. We were not able to fully assess the reliability of the judgments RPX used in making these classifications.

For the plaintiffs named in each lawsuit, Lex Machina also provided an
entity description, classifying the plaintiffs as follows:

- an operating company, or a likely operating company;
- an entity related to an operating company;
- a PME or a likely PME;
- a university;
- an individual or trust; or
- a research firm.[7]

To classify a plaintiff, Lex Machina placed more weight on statements
made by the plaintiff in official documents, such as its own court and
Securities and Exchange Commission (SEC) filings, and statements
appearing on a website maintained by the plaintiff. From these sources
Lex Machina obtained information that would help it to determine the
entity type, such as statements indicating that the plaintiff made or sold a
product or offered services, or evidence that the plaintiff shared corporate
ownership with such an entity. Some statements, such as a statement
describing a plaintiff's business as focused on patent licensing, indicated
that the plaintiff was in the business of patent monetization.

In some cases, the plaintiffs' own statements did not lead to a definitive
classification, and Lex Machina consulted other sources to obtain relevant
information about the plaintiff's business activities. To the extent possible,
Lex Machina relied on additional sources they characterized as "verified
and objective," such as corporate databases and articles of incorporation.
To the extent that Lex Machina lacked official information, it used
professional judgment to classify plaintiffs based on information from
other sources, such as news articles, blogs, court filings by opposing
parties, and Lex Machina's own database. Examples of information from
these other sources that were used to classify plaintiffs include: (1) the
number of patent infringement lawsuits filed by the plaintiff; (2) whether
the plaintiff had been sued for patent infringement in other lawsuits or
counterclaims; (3) whether the plaintiff had been subject to a declaratory
judgment lawsuit for noninfringement or invalidity; (4) the number of
defendants sued in each lawsuit and in total; (5) statements about the

---

[7]Lex Machina originally labeled these "other entity," but we determined that research firm
was a better descriptive term for these companies, although in a few cases the entity was
government sponsored.

GAO-13-465 Patent Litigation

plaintiff in news articles, blogs, or in court filings by an opposing party, such as a statement characterizing the plaintiff as a patent monetization entity; (6) whether the plaintiff was represented by an attorney known to represent patent monetization entities; and (7) evidence of linkages between the plaintiff and a patent monetization entity, such as a common principal or a street address shared in common. In some cases, the difficulty of finding information about the plaintiffs, their business activities, and their corporate relationships led Lex Machina to choose no entity classification at all. Such plaintiffs were classified as "Insufficient Evidence."

We reviewed Lex Machina's classifications of first named plaintiffs to ensure their reliability and consistency. We found 29 cases where we differed with Lex Machina's original classification. They adjusted their classifications in all but five of the cases. We agreed on different labels in these cases mainly based on our preference for the "entity related to operating company" label. Table 1 presents the evidence or information we used to review Lex Machina's classifications of first named plaintiffs.

Table 1: Evidence or Information Used to Review Lex Machina's Plaintiff Classifications

Plaintiff classification	Evidence or information used to review plaintiff classification
Operating company	The plaintiff's website, court filings, or SEC filings indicated that the plaintiff made a product, sold a product, or offered a service at the time the lawsuit was filed.
L kely operating company	In the absence of information from the plaintiff's website, court filings, or SEC filings, other sources indicated that the plaintiff made a product, sold a product, or offered a service at the time the lawsuit was filed.
Entity related to an operating company	• There was no available evidence that the plaintiff made a product, sold a product, or offered a service but there was evidence that its parent corporation, subsidiary, or other related entity made a product, sold a product, or offered a service; or • The plaintiff was a holding company that did not itself make a product, sell a product, or offer a service but owned the stock of a company that did; or • The plaintiff was a parent company to at least one subsidiary that made a product, sold a product, or offered a service; or • The plaintiff's business consisted of patent monetization but its parent, subsidiary, or other company with shared corporate ownership made a product, sold a product, or offered a service. • This category did not include plaintiffs if the only known association between it and the operating company was a licensing agreement.

Plaintiff classification	Evidence or information used to review plaintiff classification
Patent monetization entity	• The plaintiff indicated that it, or a corporate parent, was in the patent monetization business, by stating that its or its parent's purpose was to license patents or generate revenue from licensing patents; or • There was no available evidence of the plaintiff making, selling, or offering a product or service, and the plaintiff had never been sued for patent infringement, and the plaintiff had filed 8 or more patent infringement lawsuits;[a] or • There was no available evidence of the plaintiff making, selling, or offering a product or service, and the plaintiff had never been sued for patent infringement, and the plaintiff had sued a large number of defendants (around 20 or more, which put them in the top 5 percent of cases); or • There was no available evidence of the plaintiff making, selling, or offering a product or service, the plaintiff had never been sued for patent infringement, and there were at least 4 pieces of different types of other evidence supporting classification as a patent monetization entity.
Likely patent monetization entity	• There was no available evidence of the plaintiff making, selling, or offering a product or service, the plaintiff had not been sued for patent infringement, and there were 2 or 3 pieces of different types of other evidence supporting the plaintiff's classification as a patent monetization entity.
University	The plaintiff is an institution of higher education.
Individual/trust	The plaintiff identified itself in court documents as an individual or a trust.
Research firm	The plaintiff's business focus or purpose was on research and development, even if it also produced or marketed a product or service.
Insufficient evidence	• There was conflicting information about whether, at the time the lawsuit was filed, the plaintiff made or sold a product, offered a service, or was in the business of patent monetization; or • There was no more than 1 piece of other evidence supporting the plaintiff's classification as a patent monetization entity.

Source: GAO.

[a]The 106 most-asserted patents from January 2000 through February 2009 were litigated eight times or more. See John R. Allison et al., *Patent Quality and Settlement Among Repeat Patent Litigants*, 99 Geo. L. J. (2011).

In addition to steps we took to address all four objectives, to describe what is known about the key factors that contribute to recent patent litigation trends, we reviewed academic literature on the patent and judicial system and the benefits and costs of patent assertion, including economic and legal studies.

In addition to steps we took to address all four objectives, to describe developments in the judicial system that may affect patent litigation, we interviewed officials and judges from the U.S. District Courts for the District of Delaware and for the Eastern District of Texas. We selected these district courts because they had high levels of patent infringement lawsuits according to Lex Machina data. We also interviewed judges with the U.S. Court of Appeals for the Federal Circuit in Washington, D.C.,

which hears appeals of patent cases decided in federal district courts. We
also interviewed officials from the Administrative Office of the U.S. Courts
(AOUSC), and the Federal Judicial Center—organizations that provide
broad administrative, legal, and technological services and support to the
judicial branch. We also reviewed documents and data from the courts,
as well as economic and legal studies.

In addition to steps we took to address all four objectives, to describe
what actions, if any, PTO has recently taken that may affect patent
litigation in the future, we conducted interviews with officials from PTO
and reviewed documents and data from this agency, as well as economic
and legal studies.

Appendix II: Comments from the Patent and Trademark Office

UNITED STATES PATENT AND TRADEMARK OFFICE

UNDER SECRETARY OF COMMERCE FOR INTELLECTUAL PROPERTY AND
DIRECTOR OF THE UNITED STATES PATENT AND TRADEMARK OFFICE

JUL 2 6 2013

MEMORANDUM FOR Frank Rusco
Director of Natural Resources and Environment
Government Accountability Office

FROM: Teresa Stanek Rea
Acting Under Secretary and Acting Director

SUBJECT: Comments on Draft Report GAO-13-465 *"Intellectual Property --
Assessing Factors that Affect Patent Infringement Litigation Could
Help Improve Patent Quality"* (July 2013)

The United States Patent and Trademark Office (USPTO) appreciates the effort your staff has
made in your study of the consequences of patent litigation by non-practicing entities. We have
carefully reviewed and concur with the one recommendation that GAO identified in the draft
report.

GAO Recommendation: Recommend that the Secretary of Commerce direct the Acting
Director of PTO to consider examining trends in patent infringement litigation, including the
types of patents and issues in dispute, and to consider linking this information to internal data
on patent examination to improve the quality of issued patents and the patent examination
process.

USPTO Response: The USPTO appreciates GAO's recommendation. The USPTO
currently uses information relating to cases involved in patent litigation, and agrees that it
would be appropriate to consider making better use of such information by examining trends
in patent infringement litigation. The USPTO also agrees that as part of its ongoing effort to
improve the quality of issued patents and the patent examination process, it would be
appropriate to consider linking trends in patent litigation to internal data on patent
examination.

Again, we thank the Director of Natural Resources and Environment for the report. We intend to
meet the recommendations in a diligent manner, and as we move forward we will continue to
gratefully accept suggestions to help us meet the strategic goals and needs of USPTO.

Appendix III: GAO Contact and Staff Acknowledgments

GAO Contact	Frank Rusco, (202) 512-3841 or ruscof@gao.gov
Staff Acknowledgments	In addition to the individual named above, Tim Minelli (Assistant Director), Justin Fisher, Cindy Gilbert, Karen Keegan, Rob Marek, Susan Offutt, Alison O'Neill, Nalylee Padilla, Dan Royer, Susan Sawtelle, Jeanette Soares, Ardith Spence, Kiki Theodoropoulos, and Jacqueline Wade made key contributions to this report.